AF803059

£58
F/F
A 28574

GENETICS AND DNA TECHNOLOGY:

Legal Aspects

Cavendish Publishing Limited

London • Sydney

GENETICS AND DNA TECHNOLOGY:

Legal Aspects

Dr Wilson Wall
Independent Consultant Geneticist

Cavendish
Publishing
Limited

London • Sydney

First published in Great Britain 2002 by Cavendish Publishing Limited,
The Glass House, Wharton Street, London WC1X 9PX, United Kingdom
Telephone: +44 (0)20 7278 8000 Facsimile: +44 (0)20 7278 8080

Email: info@cavendishpublishing.com
Website: www.cavendishpublishing.com

© Wall, WJ 2002

All rights reserved. No part of this publication may be reproduced, stored in a retrieval system, or transmitted, in any form or by any means, electronic, mechanical, photocopying, recording, scanning or otherwise, except under the terms of the Copyrights Designs and Patents Act 1988 or under the terms of a licence issued by the Copyright Licensing Agency, 90 Tottenham Court Road, London W1P 9HE, UK, without the prior permission in writing of the publisher.

British Library Cataloguing in Publication Data

Wall, WJ (Wilson J)
Genetics and DNA technology: legal aspects
1 Genetic engineering – Law and legislation – Great Britain
I Title
344.4'1'04196

ISBN 1 85941 682 9

Printed and bound in Great Britain

CONTENTS

GLOSSARY

Allele: A version of a gene, a naturally occurring variant of a gene or DNA sequence.

Antibody: Material made by the body specifically to destroy invading antigens.

Antigen: Substance which causes an immunological reaction, such as an invading organism or foreign molecule, usually protein.

Chromosome: Individual unit in which a single molecule of DNA is wrapped around proteins. At certain times chromosomes are visible as separate entities. Humans have 46 chromosomes.

Codominant: When two alleles are present in an individual the gene product is expressed from both genes, neither is dominant or recessive.

Differential extraction: Method used to extract DNA from a sample which contains sperm and epithelial cells resulting in sperm DNA only.

DNA: Deoxyribonucleic acid, the material of heredity.

Dominant: A dominant gene is one which is preferentially expressed over a recessive gene.

Endonuclease: An enzyme which cuts DNA at specific sequences.

Founder effect: The differences between populations which are the result of having started with a small number of individuals resulting in a limited range of genetic variation within the group.

Genome: Collective noun for all the DNA in a cell or organism.

Genotype: Genetic constitution of an organism, only part of which is expressed.

Germ line cells: Cells involved in sexual reproduction that pass on genetic information from one generation to the next.

Heterozygous: Having two different versions of a gene or DNA sequence. The variants of a gene are termed alleles.

Homozygous: Having two copies of a gene, or DNA sequence, which are identical.

Linkage: Having two or more genes close together such that if one type of a gene is inherited, the other separate gene is also inherited.

Locus: A specific section of DNA, it can be part or all of an active gene, or just an anonymous section of non-coding DNA.

Mitochondrial DNA: Referred to as MtDNA. DNA inherited maternally which can be found in hair shafts and bone.

Multilocus probe: Usually abbreviated to MLP, these are sections of DNA complementary to several DNA sequences which produce a DNA profile with several bands from each MLP. See also single locus probe.

PCR: Polymerase chain reaction. A method of artificially replicating DNA in the laboratory from an original copy. When repeated several times large amounts of exact copies of a target section of DNA can be generated for further analysis.

Phenotype: The outward expression of genes.

Polymerase: Enzyme which replicates DNA.

Probe: Section of DNA which can be marked, radioactively or with a dye, and will bind to a specific piece of DNA in a sample, demonstrating its presence and size.

Recessive: A recessive gene will only be expressed in the absence of a dominant version of the gene.

Restriction: The process of enzymically cutting DNA into sections.

Short tandem repeat: Abbreviated to STR. A system used to produce a DNA profile by counting the number of repeats in a non-coding sequence of DNA. This is the current method used in most forensic applications.

Single locus probe: Usually abbreviated to SLP. Sections of DNA complementary to only one area of DNA, so when producing a DNA profile using this method it is necessary to use several SLPs.

Single nucleotide polymorphism: Abbreviated to SNP, but pronounced 'snip'. A technique used to look at single base changes in DNA. Individually they have a very low discriminatory power, but can be used collectively to produce a DNA profile.

Somatic cell: General body cell, all cells other than cells involved in sexual reproduction, the germ line cells.

INTRODUCTION

The rise in the number of expert witnesses over the last century has generally been in specialised areas unrelated to the broader areas of science. Analysis of DNA has changed this. The techniques used to produce a DNA profile are a direct use of methods devised for medical research. Similarly, previous forensic expertise is relatively easy to understand, but manipulations of DNA are both theoretically and practically very complex. A key point in this is that we, the scientists, operate within a framework of explanation and understanding which is used in a process of experiments that result in a consistent result, but since we are operating at a molecular level we cannot actually see what we are doing until the result is produced. This is not to say that there is any doubt about the way in which DNA profiles are produced, they are based on half a century of research, only that this is a direct application of an academic science.

The increasing use of DNA profiles means that they are no longer confined to murder and rape, where they originally started in 1987. The techniques have become so powerful that a DNA profile can be produced from cigarette ends and licked envelopes. It is possible to produce a profile from a single cell, a process carried out routinely as a research tool. This will no doubt become routine in forensic science also, but at the moment the very nature of crime samples makes the risk of contamination too large for single cell profiling to be practicable.

Even though much of the potential of DNA profiling has already been reached in forensic applications, there is still more which we will see over the next few years. It is in light of the current science and the still developing field of profiling that it is important that those who use this data in court have a clear grasp of the way in which it works and the results are generated. Since the first use of DNA profiling the methods used have ranged from multilocus probes (MLP), single locus probes (SLP) and currently short tandem repeat (STR) analysis. In the future we can expect to see single nucleotide polymorphism (SNP) analysis being taken into court. With these changes another laudable change has taken place. Early profiling was labour intensive and highly skilled, with results which were rather more subjective than we would ideally want. What has changed here is that automation has become the norm, taking out the high cost of labour and the subjective element of producing a result.

The manner in which results are expressed has now made it possible to generate huge numerical databases. The production of these databases will slow down the incorporation of new methods of DNA profiling because one thing that has been consistent is that every change in technology produces results which cannot be compared with results generated by the previous method. Current STR analysis is more than adequate to the task so we can assume that it will stay with us for some considerable time yet. One of the philosophical questions which production of large scale databases has raised is that of privacy, and the role of the State in balancing issues of privacy with those of security. This is a question which has become more poignant since the destruction of the World Trade Centre in New York.

In writing this book it is not my intention to provide a textbook of law; you the reader will be far more familiar with that aspect, but a resource which can be used to help understand what is done before results are taken into court. It should also help in understanding the power and the pitfalls of DNA profiles, especially the limits of what it can tell us. There is a tendency among the general public to misunderstand what a DNA profile is, some thinking that it represents the entire DNA sequence of an individual. There is also an unfortunate belief in the infallibility of DNA results. Not only are DNA profiles as prone as any complicated science to failure and mistakes, no matter how rigorous the safeguards are that are in place, but in criminal cases they are easy to misinterpret. DNA evidence, like all evidence, needs to be tempered with all the other information available. This is not the job of the scientist but a job for the court. It is the court for whom the scientist is working, whether retained by the prosecution or defence. An expert must not be partisan; an expert must try and help the court understand the results as they are presented, and this book is part of my attempt to help those who have to take DNA evidence into court understand what they are presented with.

CHAPTER 1

THE HISTORICAL CONTEXT OF PERSONAL IDENTIFICATION

INTRODUCTION

This chapter will introduce the historical context of deoxyribonucleic acid (DNA) profiling and its predecessors of personal identification: fingerprints and blood group analysis. The range of possible uses will be described, but not the techniques used to analyse body fluids. Analysis techniques will be described in later chapters. The range of different techniques of DNA analysis will be dealt with in their historical context, from the first systems, which are no longer used, to the next generation of analysis which will become available in the next few years.

Without doubt the easiest way to identify an individual is to ask them who they are, or to ask someone who knows them who they are, but in reality this is not always possible or reliable. Consequently, a great industry has arisen throughout history to find methods which could be used to pinpoint unique characteristics in an individual and therefore the individual themselves.

This developing need for reliable systems of identification seems to mirror the rise of urbanised societies. This is a result of both an increase in size of social groups, as small villages disappeared, and a reduction in social contact within the larger group. Perhaps people have more acquaintances, but fewer individuals who could be relied on to identify the person unequivocally.

Early methods of recognition relied on passwords and signs, but this only gave recognition of membership of a society or club, not recognition of the individual *per se*. The holder of the sign could still claim to be anybody they wanted to.

An effective system of identification should therefore comply with four basic features:

- for any individual it should be fixed and unalterable;
- the measured feature should be present in every individual in some form;

- ideally it should be unique to an individual;
- it should be recordable in a manner that allows for comparison.

1.1 Bertillonage

An early attempt to clearly identify an individual was made by Alphonse Bertillon (1853–1914). Both his father and brother were statisticians in France, which could well account for the direction in which the police career of Alphonse went. He was appointed the chief of the Identification Bureau in Paris. It was while there that he developed a system which came to be known as 'Bertillonage', or sometimes 'anthropometry', which he introduced in 1882. It was a useful attempt, but as we shall see, flawed by the very intractability of measuring biological systems. His system required measurements to be made of various parts of the body, and notes taken of scars and other body marks, as well as personality characteristics. These were:

- height standing;
- height sitting;
- reach from fingertip to fingertip;
- length and width of head;
- length and width of right ear;
- length of left foot;
- length of left middle finger;
- length of left little finger;
- length of left forearm.

Bertillon was also keen on the analysis of handwriting, and in 1894 he was asked to give his opinion on the origin of a handwritten document. This document was pivotal in the infamous *Dreyfus* case. Alfred Dreyfus (1859–1935) was a captain in the French army when, in 1894, circumstances resulted in a judicial error which left him imprisoned for several years. The only significant evidence was a letter, the content of which directly implicated the writer, a French officer, of betraying his country. The letter was purported to have been written by Dreyfus, an assertion which was accepted on the testimony of Alphonse Bertillon, then chief of the Identification Bureau in Paris, as an expert in handwriting. It was later shown that the incriminating document had been written by another officer. The resulting attempts at covering up the error resulted in another officer being imprisoned on a trumped-up charge, and Emile Zola being sentenced to a year's imprisonment for his now famous open letter to the President of the Republic, which started: *'J'accuse.'* Zola managed to avoid his sentence by fleeing to England. Dreyfus was eventually reinstated and was promoted to lieutenant colonel during the First World War.

Bertillonage was dogged by two related problems, both of which must be considered whenever any system of identification is being used. These two are accuracy and precision. The difference between the two is important. If repeated measurements are made on the same object, then the degree to which the results are scattered about the true value is the precision, while the closeness to the true value that the mean of the measurements comes is the accuracy.

Put another way, using the analogy of a shooting target, if the shots are spread all over the target, this is both low accuracy and low precision. If the shots are around the centre of the target, the accuracy is high but the precision low, but if shots are grouped tightly to one side of the target centre, the precision is high but the accuracy low. From this we can clearly see that it is possible to gain an accurate result from repeated measurements of low precision, as long as the measurements are not systematically distorted in one direction. This is shown diagrammatically in Figure 1.1.

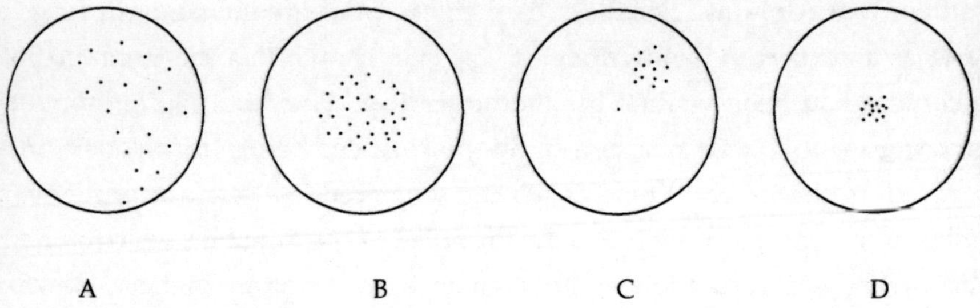

Key:
A – Large statistical and systematic error so low precision and low accuracy
B – Large statistical error but no systematic error so low precision but high accuracy
C – Small statistical error but large systematic error so high precision but low accuracy
D – Small statistical error and no systematic error so high precision and accuracy

FIGURE 1.1 Target demonstration of precision and accuracy

These two errors are also referred to as 'systematic' and 'statistical' errors. Repeated measurements can go some way to alleviate statistical errors, but systematic errors are more difficult to control as they distort the results in a single direction. Systematic errors make comparison of results from one instrument or observer to another very difficult, if not impossible, to carry out. So besides being expensive and having to specially train officers to take the Bertillonage measurements, it was also unknown what the probability of two individuals sharing the same measurements was. For these reasons, and the intrinsic lack of repeatability and complexity of measurements, it became much easier to use fingerprints and gradually replace Bertillonage completely. This resulted in fingerprints being the personal identification system of choice for over a century.

1.2 Fingerprints

The method by which fingerprints are inherited is unknown. Identical twins who share all of their DNA can be separated by their fingerprint patterns. This alone would suggest that genetic inheritance has little or nothing to do with fingerprints. However, contrary evidence suggests otherwise. Individuals with gross genetic abnormalities, that is, additional whole chromosomes as in Down's syndrome, tend to have very distinctive ridge patterns both on the fingers and palms of the hands. These are so distinctive that they alone can be used to distinguish between the few of these conditions which are compatible with life. From this we can say that there is both a genetic component and an environmental one. But how these forces interact is unknown, as is why, once formed, the pattern does not change with time or damage.

Fingerprints have a very ancient history as marks of individuality, but usually without formal measurement. The Chinese used thumbprints to verify bank notes. A thumbprint was made half on the note itself and half on the counterfoil, giving a reliable method of matching the two. The English engraver, Thomas Bewick, was sufficiently impressed by the delicate tracery of his fingerprints that he produced engravings of two of his fingertips and used them as signatures to his work.

The constancy of fingerprints was first described by Johannes Purkinje, a Czech scientist, in a paper he read at a scientific meeting in 1823. It was, however, much later that the foundation of modern fingerprinting was laid down with the publication in 1892 of *Finger Prints* (London: HMSO), by Sir Francis Galton. Before this, in 1870, one of the first reliable uses of fingerprinting in the solving of a crime was made. A Scottish physician, by the name of Henry Faulds, amassed a large collection of fingerprints while working in Tokyo. Knowing of his interest and expertise, he was asked to help in solving a crime where a sooty fingerprint had been left by the perpetrator. Faulds was able to demonstrate that the man originally arrested for the crime was innocent. When another suspect was arrested, he showed that his fingerprints matched those left at the scene. While the method used by Faulds was deemed adequate at the time, it was quickly realised that formalising both the methods of fingerprint analysis, and the principles upon which it was based, was of significant importance. In 1902 the London Metropolitan Police set up the Central Fingerprint Branch, and by the end of that year 1,722 identifications had been made.

The idea that every contact between two objects leaves a trace is sometime called Locard's Principle, after Edmond Locard, who first formalised the idea. Locard (1877–1966) was a forensic scientist in France and a renowned fingerprint expert. This can be extended beyond fingerprints to cover any material from an assailant recovered from the victim, either as a result of resistance, as in the case of blood or skin scratched from the attacker, or as in the case of rape, semen left as a direct result of the assault. This, however, is probably as far as the use of such a principle should go, since it can easily be imagined that contact between two non-shedding surfaces, such as some man-made materials, would not leave a trace. There is also the question of traces left in such small quantities that they are beyond the power of detection using contemporary methods. Fingerprints represent a form of detectable transfer evidence.

1.2.1 The nature of fingerprints

Broadly speaking, the ridge patterns found on fingertips come in three forms, with a recognised frequency in the population. It is worth noting that individuals with abnormal chromosome complements, such as Down's syndrome, have a very different frequency of ridge pattern which can be used as an aid to diagnosis of the condition. The different types and normal frequencies are:

- loops (70%);
- whorls (25%);
- arches (5%).

These different pattern types are shown in Figure 1.2.

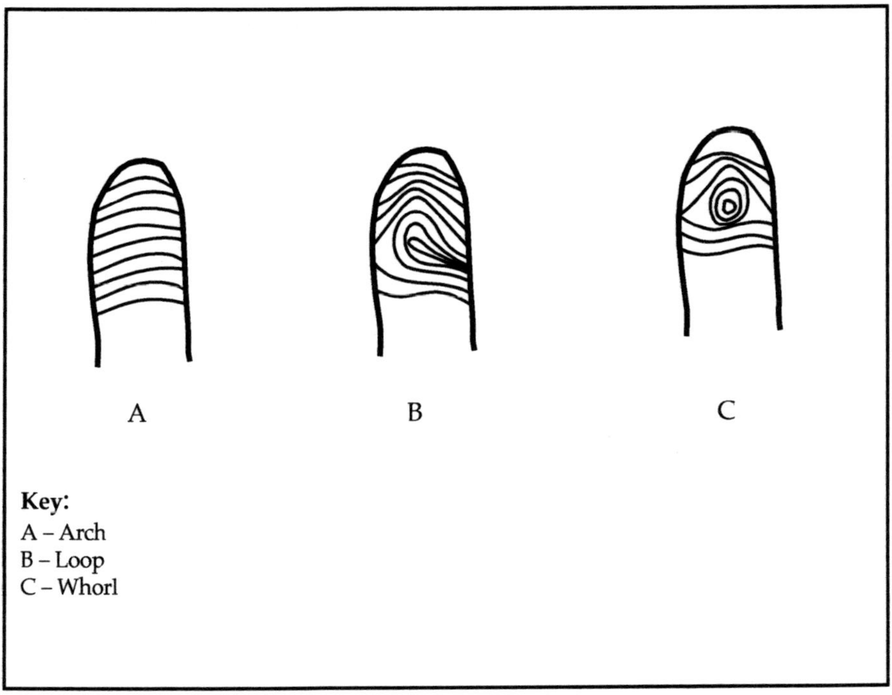

FIGURE 1.2 Fingertip dermatoglyphs

The seemingly straightforward nature of fingerprints should be looked at with an open mind because, as we shall see, results are not always unambiguous.

Most countries maintain collections of fingerprints, which serve two purposes. The first is to identify an individual so that they can be associated with past convictions and to determine if they are required to answer further charges associated with other crimes; the second is to find out whether marks left at a crime scene can be associated with a known person, and therefore reduce the number of suspects that need to be looked for.

When comparing a fingerprint, or set of prints, from an individual with a set of records in a database, it is normal to have a good, clear set of prints in the collection from a previous encounter as well as a clear set of prints from the individual to be compared with the database. The difficulties arise with the comparison of a scene of crime mark with a database. This is essentially complicated because the mark will usually be partial or smudged, so that only certain features can be compared. The process is assisted by the use of computers once the characteristics of a fingerprint have been designated by a fingerprint expert. It is the convention of characterising fingerprints, and their underlying assumptions, which might give cause for concern.

The first thing we should remember about any method of personal identification is that unless it has adequate discriminatory power it will not perform the job. Fingerprints are very good at separating individuals, of that there is no doubt, but there are two questions which are asked about fingerprints which we should consider before looking at the various systems of measurement of them which are commonly used. The first of these questions is 'are fingerprints unique?' and the second is 'how many different fingerprints are there?' It may seem that these are somehow contradictory, for if there is a number which can be put to the range of different fingerprints, a fingerprint cannot be unique. Similarly, if a fingerprint is unique then it would be reasonable to assume that there is an infinite range of fingerprints possible. However, if we take these two questions separately it is possible to show that both can be answered without contradiction.

Is a fingerprint unique? There are two answers to this. At any given time it is probably true to say that no two people share the same fingerprint, so in a temporal sense they are unique. But in absolute terms they are most definitely not. There are also two reasons for this – one is that the possibility of two people sharing a fingerprint by chance alone cannot be absolutely ruled out, and the second reason bears on our other question: how many fingerprints are possible? For this we have to realise that, contrary to common belief, there is not an infinite variety of fingerprints available. To understand this we need to think a little more about the difference between a large number and infinity. Infinity is essentially a mathematical construct, and it really has no place in our physical world. We can say that a straight line is the circumference of a circle of infinite radius, but no such circle exists. On the other hand, even if all the atoms in the universe were rearranged in all the different ways possible, there would still not be an infinite number of permutations. The number would be very large, indeed incalculably large, but it would still be a number, a finite figure. So, in a finger of finite dimensions (however big or small it is) there is a finite number of atoms, and even if we could detect the difference of a single atom there would still be a finite number of different fingerprints possible. To bring this down to more manageable levels, it is only the ridges which are looked at on a fingerprint, with the result that there is very definitely a fixed number of possibilities available. Since fingerprint comparisons are made subjectively, only using certain features, the possibility of similar fingerprints being mistakenly thought to have come from the same person becomes a much more realistic one.

When using fingerprints for identification, they are normally classified into basic patterns, as shown in Figure 1.2, with the addition of compounds of these patterns and consideration of any scarring that may be present. After this, the ridge count between features can be used, although it is the gap between ridges which is counted as these tend to be pressure independent, so while the distance between features might change with the pressure exerted by the finger leaving the print, the ridge count will not. While features, also called *typica*, may vary from system to system, for any database of fingerprints to be useful it must at least be consistent in what are defined as features. Some of these are shown in Figure 1.3, although this should not be taken as a definitive listing.

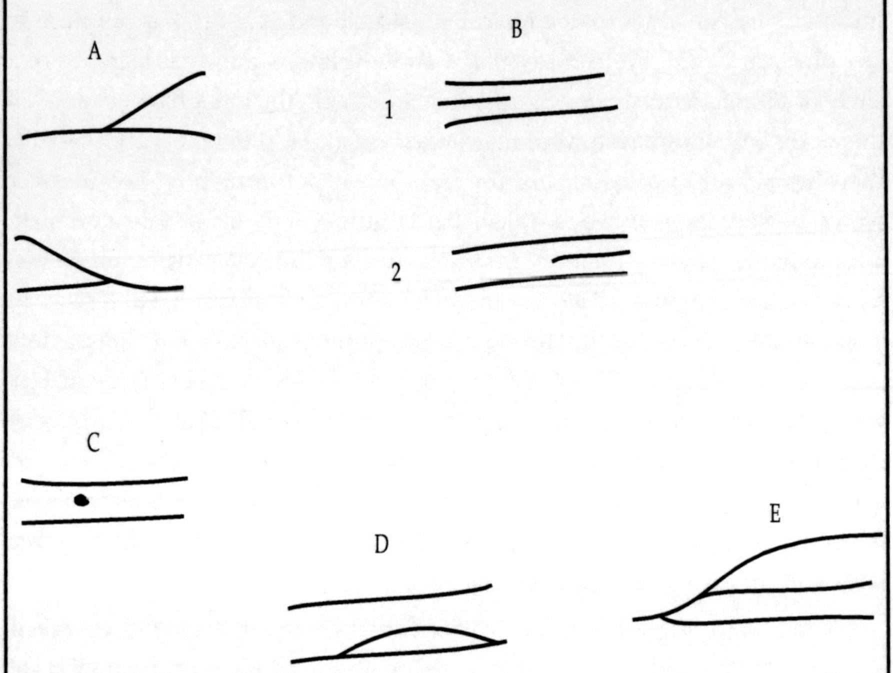

Key:
A – Forks (1) right fork (2) left fork
B – Ridges (1) ending left (2) ending right
C – Dot
D – Island
E – Trifurcation

FIGURE 1.3 Features commonly used in defining a fingerprint

By measuring features relative to each other a numerical picture can be created which can be compared from print to print. Different countries use different systems to evaluate fingerprints for comparison. For example, the Netherlands uses 12 points while the UK uses 16 points. By assuming that features originate effectively at random and are not related, it is possible to generate databases of tens of millions of fingerprints, all of which are different using these systems. There is no doubt that great weight is given to fingerprint evidence, and quite rightly so, but as we shall discuss next, there is still a need for caution when faced with this evidence because interpretation is not necessarily exact or entirely objective.

It is in the realm of practical analysis where problems may arise with fingerprints. Two imprints from the same finger may ostensibly differ quite markedly because of the pressure with which they were made, of the amount of material already on the finger obscuring the ridges, or when a formal fingerprint is taken, the amount of ink used. This potential variation in the fingerprint, and therefore its interpretation, can be most clearly seen in considering the *typica* termed a 'dot and ridge' ending. Unless the print is of very high quality, not only could a dot disappear, but a dot could be artificially produced by a ridge end having a stutter. To help in this it is normal to allow for a match to be declared by the fingerprinter. Using the skill of the fingerprinter to decide matches between features is, therefore, being perhaps a little more subjective than would necessarily be desirable.

Fingerprint evidence has developed a sense of infallibility which is not wholly justified. While the number of matching points on a fingerprint is set down, the decision as to whether a match between two points is valid rests with the fingerprint specialist. It is not necessary for the fingerprint technician to understand the theoretical basis of his work to produce a result which can be taken into court and, as we shall see when we deal in detail with DNA evidence, this is also true of far more complex systems. But it has been pointed out that although there is no absolute value for the number of matching points which are needed for declaring, in the opinion of the fingerprinter, that two fingerprints match, it remains a matter of opinion. There is also a scientific debate about fingerprints which may seem academic, but does raise suspicions in scientific circles. Without a calculated error rate, that is, incorrectly declared matches and incorrectly declared exclusions, it is virtually impossible to regard a set of results as reliable. Not stating an error rate is not the same as a zero error rate, which would in itself be highly suspicious.

This has two potentially conflicting results. The first is that it may be possible to challenge the opinion of one expert with that of another, and the second is that not having enough matching points may deprive the court of probative information. Fingerprints are rarely taken in isolation, so it could be said that a partial print, not necessarily conforming to an arbitrarily set standard, may give additional information to the court in assessing a case. However, even if the fingerprint expert can demonstrate a clear understanding of the theory of point matching and construction of probabilities, because such standards are set, not adhering to them could be seen as an invitation to contest the result by the provision of an alternative fingerprint expert.

All of these arguments lead us to consider the possibility that point matching is a form of numerical tyranny, giving an objective veneer to what is essentially a matter of opinion. There is nothing wrong with relying upon opinion, so long as every opinion is a result of the same training, which is based on the same clear theoretical basis. Unfortunately, people differ and so do their opinions. So although the number of points of match is regarded as the lynchpin of reliability in fingerprints, opinions may well differ as to the number of points which need to match.

It may be that it would be desirable to automate the process of fingerprint identification. This has been tried before, but with limited success, the failure not being associated with the performance of the available computers, but with the way in which the problem is dealt with by the software. Similar dynamic problems of identification have been dealt with both in speech recognition and handwriting interpretation. The advent of software based on neural networks, which are very much more complicated than the more usual software algorithms, could solve the problem of consistency and finally bring a level of objectivity into the use of fingerprints which has not previously been possible. It remains to be seen whether such a utopian ideal is possible, but it should be worked towards because the evidential value of fingerprints is immense and will remain so. It should also be remembered that other patterns and indentations left behind, such as teeth marks, footprints and gloveprints, all have the same potential for automated analysis, but can be even more subjective in interpretation at the moment.

1.3 Blood groups and other proteins

Alternative methods of personal identification primarily stem from work carried out for the purposes of medical research. Although blood groups were worked out at the very beginning of the 20th century, the start of the story was much earlier, with the first attempts at blood transfusions. It would be reasonable to assume that blood transfusions as we know them could not have been carried out before there was a clear understanding of blood as a circulating material, rather than the earlier ebb-and-flow model. A frequently cited first transfusion was of Pope Innocent VIII in 1492, although the possibility of this being a true transfusion is unlikely since William Harvey did not describe his model of blood circulation until 1628. Over the next few years energetic attempts were made at introducing various chemicals into the circulation, but it was many years before reliable accounts of the transfer of blood from one organism to another can be found. An early authentic example is attributed to Richard Lord, who transferred blood from one dog to another. Two years later he infused a man, described as healthy but mildly insane, with blood from a lamb. His survival is remarkable because cross-species transfusions are usually fatal. Indeed, such were the problems associated with the technique that many countries in Europe banned the operation completely. By the 19th century the use of non-animal, that is, human donors was recognised as the only practical solution to the problem of killing the patient, but lack of knowledge of blood groups still caused such difficulties that transfusion was only attempted as a last resort. As an alternative, salt solutions were used to replace blood as transfusable material which, although safe in comparison with alien blood, was administered in such a haphazard fashion that problems still arose, the point being that if the salt solution is too dilute it will cause the blood cells to rupture, and if it is too strong the blood cells will collapse.

The turning point for blood transfusions, and incidentally for personal identification, came with the publication by Karl Landsteiner of his description of blood cell agglutination in 1901. Landsteiner was to receive a Nobel Prize for this work in 1930. He had trouble believing his own results because they ran counter to the current thinking of the time. In fact, it was not until 1908 that a straightforward model of inheritance was suggested, and a further two years before this idea was clearly demonstrated.

Blood groups are essentially designated by marker molecules on the surface of red blood cells, and the precise nature of these and their uses will be dealt with in detail in a later chapter. The important aspect of blood groups in forensic applications is their discriminatory power. Blood grouping tests have not significantly changed in the years since their introduction, because they represent a very simple system which, although powerful at the time of its introduction, is comparatively limited when compared with later technology. When Landsteiner started his systematic investigation, it was already known that red blood cells would stick together under certain circumstances, but until his work this phenomenon was only used as a diagnostic in typhoid fever. Landsteiner originally described his blood groups as A, B and C (now O), and it was eight years later that that blood group AB was described by one of his students.

One of the insights which Landsteiner had about the individuality of blood groups was precisely that – they were individual. In this simple form they were, it had to be admitted, of low discriminatory power, but they would be augmented with other systems later. In 1903 Landsteiner published a report on the potential of blood groups to be used in forensic applications. To do this he compared his blood typing results from fresh blood with those of blood dried onto glass, linen and wood. As would be expected, the dried material did not produce a result as clear as the fresh material, but it produced a result nonetheless. Having used an independent observer for these typing experiments he was convinced as to the efficacy of the system for forensic applications. By the 1920s ABO blood grouping was routinely used on patients being given blood transfusions, thereby reducing the mortality rate. The molecules which give rise to the blood groups are called antigens, and are surprisingly common in nature, being frequently found in foods and micro-organisms which colonise humans, as well as our sweat and tears.

Using simple ABO blood groups, and the gradual discovery of new and different blood typing systems, has increased the discriminatory power of blood groups in forensic applications quite considerably, but nowhere near the discriminatory power of DNA analysis. The increased performance of blood grouping, and exactly how it works, will be dealt with in detail in Chapter 3.

1.4 DNA analysis

There was a considerable time lag between using variations in blood groups and the analysis of DNA directly. This was not because the potential of DNA analysis was not recognised, but because direct analysis of DNA was not possible. While blood groups were recognised and used from the early part of the 20th century, this was carried out with no clear understanding of how they came about, were controlled, or inherited. Although it had long been known that cell nuclei were important in inheritance, which component was actually responsible remained a mystery. Using relatively simple methods of chemical analysis it was possible to distinguish two major components of cell nuclei. The first was proteins and the second was nucleic acid. At this point it is worth remembering that proteins are very complicated molecules with intricate three dimensional structures, while DNA is a long, linear molecule made up of four simple building blocks arranged in apparently random order down the length of the molecule. A logical argument which ran along the following lines was used to try and decide if it was protein or DNA which was the stuff of heredity. Since organisms are complex, a simple molecule such as DNA could not possibly carry all the necessary information of heredity; it would take a complex molecule to do that, therefore it must be the complex proteins which carry the genetic information. As we now know, this argument is false and DNA is the genetic data carrier, but it was 1940 before experiments were conducted to prove it. So, by the second half of the 20th century it was known that DNA was the coding material for life, but very little else about it. This changed in 1953, when Watson and Crick proposed their now famous double helix model of DNA structure, for which they received a Nobel Prize. But there were still no practical uses to which this knowledge could be put; forensic applications of DNA remained in the realm of the indirect testing of DNA in the form of blood groups and other proteins. These are under direct control of DNA, but one step removed from it – the grail of direct DNA analysis was still a long way off.

The realisation that DNA itself could be used in forensic applications was a direct spin-off from medical research, although the speed with which it was picked up by the forensic community was admirable. The breakthrough came in 1984, when Alec Jeffreys made a fortuitous observation while looking for disease markers, that is, identifiable sections of DNA which are inherited with an unknown disease gene: some of these markers were highly variable, thereby producing a highly discriminatory system for identifying individuals.

Although one of the first forensic applications was in a criminal case, this was not the only application for which it was considered. An early aspect was in the identification of bodies, and for very good reasons.

When a body is found that has no immediately apparent means of identification, such as documents, the task is to try and find out who the person was. This may be for purely humanitarian reasons, but also so that next of kin can be informed. This is not always as easy as it might sound; there was, for example, an unidentified body after the fire at Kings Cross Station, London. There is also the question of malicious disposal of a body, frequently in different pieces. In such circumstances, it is necessary to find out how many bodies are involved; after all, if two arms and a leg are recovered from a river it can be extremely difficult to know for certain if these parts represent one, two or three people. Similarly, it may not be possible to clearly identify bodies or body parts after a severe fire or accident, such as an aeroplane crash. Traditional techniques of fingerprinting and blood group analysis may not help in answering questions of identity under these circumstances.

Fire will quickly remove skin and, therefore, fingerprints, as will prolonged immersion in water, but it is also obvious that trying to identify an unknown body from fingerprints presupposes that the individual has a record of their fingerprints available for comparison. What is possible using blood groups and other protein markers is the construction of family trees, which can place an individual within a family, but blood groups are broken down relatively quickly in the environment and so they may not be of any use. Whatever the technique employed, it generally has a starting point of a missing person report. If there are no other telling signs, such as documents or a recognisable body, then it becomes necessary to utilise the new techniques of DNA analysis.

Methods of DNA analysis have changed quite considerably since the first practical application of the technique in the mid-1980s, but what is retained from technique to technique is the need for a considerable investment in equipment and manpower. DNA analysis is far more expensive than fingerprint or blood group analysis, where reagents are relatively cheap and the process relatively fast to carry out, in comparison.

The first use in the UK of DNA analysis was carried out in Leicestershire. In October 1987 a youth was charged with the sexual assault and murder of a teenage girl in a Leicestershire village. It was suspected that the same youth was responsible for another sexual assault and murder that had been carried out three years earlier. Semen left behind on the victim provided enough DNA for a profile to be produced. The profiles from the two assaults demonstrated two important points: the first was that the arrested youth could be completely ruled out as the assailant, and the second was that, given the limits of the statistics, the two assaults were carried out by the same individual. This second point is particularly important, because there was no clear understanding at that time of the possible limitations and power of this technique. The statistical basis upon which the profiles would come to rely in court had not been fully worked out; arguments would rage for many years to come on the statistical and biological bases of these tests.

As a result of the implications arising from the DNA profiles produced in this original case, it was quickly realised that another individual must be sought. So in January 1987 an unprecedented decision was made by the Leicestershire police force – because it was thought that the assailant was a local man, and the village concerned was relatively small, they asked all the males in the community to voluntarily give blood for a mass screening. Because the number of people who could be screened was approximately 5,000, it would have been totally impractical to produce a DNA profile from each one and compare it with the profile from the semen. Therefore, to make the task easier an initial screen was carried out, using the faster and cheaper, but much less discriminatory, technique of blood grouping.

After this preliminary screening approximately 500 individuals were left. This was a much more manageable number of DNA tests to carry out, but still a very large number for the testing laboratory. The initial hope that this systematic approach would result in either a smaller number of individuals to be investigated, or better still, a single individual, was quickly dashed. No matches were found. The assailant was eventually picked up because he could not help boasting that he had paid a friend to give blood on his behalf. This raised questions regarding the chain of custody of samples, especially when an individual is trying to avoid identification for whatever reason, and has considerable importance in paternity disputes (Home Office Circular No 91/1989, *Blood Testing in Paternity Cases; Choice of Tester*).

When biopsy samples are taken during surgical procedures for histological examination, it is quite normal for the remaining sample to be retained, usually embedded in wax. These are fertile sources of DNA for testing, as are dried and preserved foods or, in the case of Egyptian mummies, whole bodies. Mummified remains can often be used to produce entire DNA profiles which can be used to create family trees from a collection of ancient individuals. Another source of resilient DNA is bone marrow. Because the long bones of humans, such as the thigh bones and arm bones, contain active bone marrow which produces blood cells, they also contain large amounts of cellular DNA. This is very well protected within the cavity of the bones and, consequently, is also highly resistant to bacterial decay. It is the bone marrow within these long bones which is the last area to be destroyed by decay in buried bodies. While the soft tissues can disappear quite quickly, and with them their DNA, bone marrow is very well protected and can last several years, depending of course on the environmental conditions prevailing at the time. Although it is unusual for decomposition of biological material to take place without the aid of bacteria or fungi, cooking and eating meat will break down both protein and DNA into their component parts in a very similar way to bacterial degradation, but using human enzymes as well as bacteria in the gut.

This problem of identifying human remains was demonstrated in a case which started in 1981, when a 15 year old girl disappeared. Eight years later, in 1989, the remains of the girl were found and it was confirmed as murder. Inevitably, these remains were in a very bad state of decay. Initially, identification was made based on facial reconstruction and dental records, this being possible because matching age and sex to missing persons allowed the search to be narrowed down. Final confirmation was only achieved when a family tree was constructed, based on DNA profiles of the family, and DNA from the body was put into the picture.

In a similar way, it has been attempted to associate an individual with a crime after their death. This has proved more difficult, but exhumations can be used successfully when the burial has taken place not too many years previously. It is not possible to be precise about the length of time after which exhumation will yield analysable DNA. The prevailing environmental conditions are the controlling factor in this. At the two extremes would be burial in permafrost, leaving a permanently frozen body, or desert sand, which would dry out and mummify the body. In between these two is a range of conditions which would decompose the body at differing rates, depending on temperature and presence of water.

The number of different methods which are available for DNA analysis is considerable, but very few are used in forensic applications. There are many reasons for this, primarily amongst these is that some systems need far more DNA for the analysis than is often available. Other factors include cost and expertise of the analyst and the speed with which it can be carried out. One aspect that has played an important role in deciding which systems to use for routine DNA analysis is that of the associated statistical analysis.

There would be little purpose in taking a DNA profile into court and declaring a match without some demonstrable proof that it is unlikely that another individual shares the same profile. It is also true that some systems of DNA analysis produce results which are so complicated that the results are not easy to express in an understandable form and, although highly discriminatory, would require prohibitively large computers to produce a useable database.

Perhaps one of the most valuable aspects of DNA analysis is that not only can the results be relatively straightforward to express, and therefore easily computerised, but the original analysis can be automated. This is particularly important because, as we have seen with fingerprinting, an element of subjectivity can easily creep into analysis of biological material, whether an imprint or biological material. Early methods of DNA analysis using probes were not easily automated because of the way in which results were produced. They were effectively analysed by a simple comparison of test results.

One of the reasons that computerisation of early techniques did not work was that there was little agreement as to how precise and accurate the technique was. While it was possible to set up consistent methods of results comparison, it was not always clear at what point the results would be regarded as different. Different laboratories had different standards. This became a particular problem when it was realised that it was simply not possible to compare results between different laboratories, so all testing had to be carried out at a single site and at the same time, to make any sense at all.

It was, therefore, with some considerable relief that these first techniques of single locus probe (SLP) and multilocus probes (MLP) were abandoned in the early 1990s in favour of short tandem repeat (STR) analysis. In later chapters details will be given as to the methods and practical pitfalls of SLP and MLP analysis, even though they are rarely used in forensic laboratories any more. Short tandem repeat analysis is carried out in a quite different way to previous systems, and is effectively automated from the point at which DNA is extracted from the sample to the production of the results. In broad terms, this solves the question of subjectivity but, as we shall see, not entirely. Any machine based errors, on the other hand, should at least be consistent.

Short tandem repeat analysis is the current method of choice in forensic cases. It is a relatively quick method of DNA analysis, and although it requires a large capital outlay for equipment, a large throughput of samples is possible, with unattended equipment running overnight.

1.5 New methods of DNA analysis for the future

It should not be imagined that analysis of DNA has reached a plateau, or fullstop, in development. In the last quarter of the 20th century all the methods of DNA analysis used for forensic applications looked at very small areas of the total human genome. The size of the sections looked at has varied as techniques have changed, but the total variation which is used is still a tiny fraction of the whole human genome. In many ways this is wasting a resource, but it may never be possible, or desirable, to sequence the entire genome of an individual. It may not be possible because, as far as we can tell at the moment, it would require enormous amounts of DNA to carry out. Even if the technology were available, such would be the scale of the task that even a fraction of 1% error would render the results useless. It is often not fully realised that the Human Genome Project, which aims to sequence the entire human genome, essentially operates on a consensus principle because variation can be found in the genome in all manner of ways. In Chapter 2 a more detailed review of DNA will be given.

Given that sequencing is unlikely to become a useable forensic tool, the question remains: where will forensic DNA analysis go? The most likely answer to this is in the form of analysis of single nucleotide polymorphisms

(SNPs – pronounced 'snips'). Study of SNPs developed, like so many other techniques, as a method to speed up and extend the possibilities of genetic diagnosis. SNP analysis is carried out by looking for very small changes in the genome – in fact, single base changes to the chemical structure of DNA. It is for this reason that SNPs are relatively uninformative on their own, but when a large panel is used made up of tens of these, all of which are different, the discriminatory power is correspondingly multiplied. The difference between this technique and the current one of short tandem repeat (STR) analysis is that, instead of counting the number of repeat sequences, as in the case of STRs, SNP analysis looks for a single chemical change to DNA. It can be readily appreciated that there is little or no scientific advantage to SNP analysis compared with STR analysis, but there is one major advantage – technology. STR analysis uses a lot of time and equipment to carry out, but SNP analysis is different: because it has so many different applications beyond simple forensics, commercial pressure has developed it quickly to the point of being ready for validation and then use. The method of SNP analysis has also been developed in a quite different way; it should be possible to carry out the test quickly and easily, with the result readable in a very short time. Certainly it is envisaged that for medical diagnostics using SNP, it should be possible to carry out the whole procedure in a doctor's surgery. Although this belies the technology and research that has been put into this type of DNA analysis over many years, the forensic community will no doubt benefit from it.

SUMMARY

Methods of personal identification have changed immensely in the last 150 years. The first systems used by police were subjective in the extreme, but were gradually replaced by better systems. The first method used successfully was fingerprinting, but having started as a clear method of identification, it turned into a system for tracking down individuals from prints left at the scene of a crime. While few, if anybody, would dispute that a clear set of 10 fingerprints will identify an individual, there is some controversy surrounding the use of partial prints and declared matches from a few *typica* from a smudged fingerprint. While it is often claimed that fingerprints are unique, this is not a claim ever made about the next great step forward in identification: blood groups. These have one great advantage over fingerprints – they can be used in paternity disputes, as their mode of inheritance is well known and consequently can be traced through generations. Blood groups have a relatively low discriminatory power in forensic applications, but nonetheless have been of considerable value. When genetics became a 'hard' science, rather than a descriptive natural history, in the second half of the 20th century a great leap forward was made in forensic applications. Although still not regarded as unique, identical twins share exactly the same DNA and therefore DNA profiles, and the discriminatory power of DNA analysis makes it ideal for paternity cases and criminal cases of all sorts, in fact, any case where biological material has been left behind. This can be anything from an obvious bloodstain to a cigarette end, or a licked envelope flap. The methods of DNA analysis have themselves changed, from very intricate and complicated techniques requiring highly skilled scientists, to automated systems that have a very high turnover, making the compilation of huge amounts of data not only feasible but possible.

CHAPTER 2

AN IDEAL SAMPLE

INTRODUCTION

The starting point for any analysis is a sample, of course, but the nature of the sample can determine what sort of analysis can be carried out and what sort of results can be expected. Although it can be very easy to produce some sort of a result from any sample, the interpretation of that result depends on several fundamental questions:

- Is it the right sample for the analysis?
- Can the sample be analysed at all?
- Is the fundamental science behind the analysis sufficiently understood for the results to be held as valid?
- To what degree can errors in sample handling affect test results?
- What is an acceptable level of error for the analysis of the sample?

Although not an exhaustive list of questions to be answered, these few give a good indication of the potential pitfalls of any new system when first introduced. An interesting point here is that, although the fundamental science behind a process may be well established and understood, it is not necessary for the technician to have that knowledge. It is adequate that the laboratory manager has a grasp of all the particulars, as without it a laboratory can slip into sloppy working practices through a lack of understanding. A possibly trivial example of lack of understanding resulting in poor practice takes place in most offices. Have you ever wondered why the base plate on a stapler can be rotated so that the staple pins are pushed outwards rather than inwards? It is so that the staple can emulate the use of a pin holding documents together and, just like a pin, it becomes possible to unstaple papers or cheques from documents with no more trouble than removing a pin. I have yet to receive any documents which need to be separated that have been correctly stapled. This knowledge seems to have been all but lost, although it aids the handling of documents. More stringently, activities carried out in a laboratory have to be carefully monitored so that short cuts are not introduced which compromise the result.

The safe processing of samples starts with an understanding of what the sample is, what it represents and what the test process is going to do to it.

2.1 Structure of DNA

DNA is found in all human cells except red blood cells, being confined to the nucleus, and a few smaller cellular inclusions called mitochondria. When a DNA profile is carried out on blood it is the white blood cells which are used, not the red blood cells. However, when blood grouping is carried out, it is the red blood cells which are tested; although they have no DNA of their own, the blood groups are controlled by the DNA in the stem cells which give rise to them.

DNA is a long molecule, effectively a chain of small repeated sub-units. In humans DNA occurs as 46 separate units, each one wound up into a chromosome. Chromosomes are important biologically as they control DNA so that only the right genes are used at any given time. When producing a DNA profile, the first thing that is done is that the chromosomes are disrupted so that there are 46 individual molecules of DNA originating from every cell. Genes are sections of DNA which code for molecules that carry out specific functions within the cell. The sub-units of DNA which are so important are of four different types: adenine, cytosine, guanine and thymine. These are normally abbreviated to A, C, G and T. When strung out in the form of DNA, attached to a structural backbone, they appear as a random string of letters, but this appearance is deceptive. The letters of DNA are read in groups of three, and every triplet code defines some aspect of protein synthesis.

By having two strands of DNA which follow a simple pairing rule, the classical double helix is produced. The pairing rule is simple: A pairs opposite T, and G pairs opposite C. These are the only stable configurations and are demonstrated by a simple string:

ATATCTGATGCATACGTACTGTAGGCATCGTCAACGTA

TATAGACTACGTATGCATGACATCCGTAGCAGTTGCAT

These gene sequences are not usually the ones which are used to produce a DNA profile, for a very simple reason. Consider the situation in which comparison was to be made between the DNA sequence of the same gene from two different individuals. For this example, the gene being tested in our sample is a gene which is important to every individual, such as insulin. So when we look at sections of the gene what we see is identical DNA between individuals and so, as a forensic tool in identification, is next to useless. This hypothetical situation can be extended into reality. Some gene sequences code for proteins which are so fundamental to the healthy functioning of the cell that there is virtually no variation in the DNA sequence throughout the animal kingdom. It is true to say that approximately 98% of the human genome is held in common with the mouse. This does not of course mean that we are only 2% away from being mice; the picture for geneticists is far more complicated than that, in the same way that describing a car in generic terms applies to all cars, but the manner in which the parts interact makes them different.

So when we want to test a sample to create a DNA profile, we use sections of DNA found both between genes and, in some instances, within genes, which do not code for anything themselves and are therefore free to vary and alter over time without disturbing the integrity of the cell. The precise sort of variation will be looked at in more detail in Chapter 4 dealing with the way in which results are produced and reported.

It can be clearly seen from this that a sample for DNA analysis differs from one being used for blood grouping. Blood groups are a direct product of genetics, as will be discussed in more detail in Chapter 3, and so they would not be expected to show the same range of variation, and therefore discriminatory power, of DNA analysis. This is exactly what is found, so we can say that any analysis of a sample involving either a functional gene or a gene product will produce a result of low probity, if any at all.

2.2 Minimum requirements for a forensic sample

The staggering sensitivity of current DNA analysis techniques, which can produce a result from a single cell, can be seen to be at the maximum theoretical sensitivity of DNA analysis. However, issues surround the current ability of the systems used to produce a result which can be relied upon with these minimal amounts of DNA.

To produce a result from a single cell is in itself quite extraordinary, for the following reason. Every cell in the human body, with the exception of sperm and eggs, contains two copies of nearly all the genes. It has to be said that it is nearly all because some genes are only to be found on one of the sex chromosomes. Sex chromosomes are the only ones which are not found as a similar pair: females have two identical sex chromosomes (designated X) and males have two very dissimilar sex chromosomes (designated X and Y). The use of X and Y is purely historical, and does not refer to the shape of the chromosomes. X was used because early geneticist saw a mysterious dark area of nuclei – hence X. When it was later realised what the X body was, the next logical step was to call the male determining chromosome Y. Sex determination is different in other organisms so, for example, in birds the sex chromosomes are called Z and W. So females who have two sex chromosomes the same have two copies of every gene, while males have only one copy of the many thousands of genes which reside on the X chromosome, there being virtually nothing genetically active on the Y chromosome except that which makes for maleness. With two copies of all the DNA which is currently tested in forensic applications in every cell, it is reasonable to assume that analysing DNA from a single cell at least allows for two copies to be present. However, it is possible to analyse DNA from a single sperm, though this is not an easy procedure because the sample in such a case is a cell with only half the normal DNA content. Even given the ability to carry out such a procedure on a routine basis, it would not be sensible to do so for the very good reason that each sperm would contain only a partial profile containing a range of values which would make interpretation extremely difficult. When semen samples are collected for analysis, by having a large number of sperm cells present to analyse, an overall picture emerges which represents the true DNA profile.

Samples used in criminal investigations are either from a scene of crime or a comparison sample. Comparison samples are most frequently blood samples, although nasal swabs, mouth washes, mouth swabs or plucked hairs will all serve the purpose just as well as blood. Indeed, with the increasing awareness of hazards associated with handling blood it is surprising that more use is not made of the non-invasive collection of samples for DNA analysis.

Whatever sample type is used, it is generally accepted that a lower limit for forensic analysis should be the mass of DNA present in approximately 1,000 cells. This is still a very small amount, but it is enough for a sound and reliable result, and it is a thousand times more than the smallest amount theoretically analysable. This has resulted in a reliable method of producing a result from such items as cigarette ends, and licked stamps and envelope flaps. The increasing use of self-adhesive envelopes and stamps will ultimately reduce the value of this sort of analysis, but no doubt other sources of DNA will be found which can be satisfactorily analysed.

Quantities of this small size test the system of careful handling to its limits because, although not always realised, these samples are too small to be seen with the naked eye. Indeed, once a DNA sample is in solution and ready for analysis it is only at the stage of the final result that it is certain that any DNA was present. Because of this, it is essential that adequate safeguards are in place so that inadvertent contamination can be ruled out and the test has worked, even if no result has been produced. These are referred to as 'controls' and are designed so that they always produce the same result, so if the controls produce unexpected results the entire test is declared void. Some controls contain known DNA, so if these produce a correct result the test has worked. Other controls contain all the reagents necessary for the test except DNA. These should not produce a result. If both of these controls produce the expected outcome, then it is assumed that whatever the result is originating from the test sample, it is a true reflection of what was actually there.

2.3 Errors arising from the sample

While gross errors in testing can create a result which is obviously incorrect, some errors are not so easily controlled but may still be significant. It is a common assumption that DNA evidence is clear-cut, and that the result of analysis is certain. Unfortunately this is not so. We shall deal with the aspects of errors specifically associated with the process of analysis and at how errors in the sample itself can affect the outcome of analysis.

In this context we can describe an error as anything which alters the outcome of the analysis, whether randomly or directionally. A random error might give false positives or false negatives, while a directional, or systematic, error will prejudice a result in one direction only, resulting in a tendency to false negative or false positive results only.

There are many ways in which a sample can introduce errors into a system, some of them obvious and straightforward to guard against, and some more difficult to recognise and even more difficult to contain. Errors can be introduced accidentally or deliberately, or may be an intrinsic part of the sample itself.

2.3.1 Deliberate introduction of errors

Errors which are deliberately introduced into a sample are generally of a malicious nature. They can range in form from an individual persuading another person to give a sample on their behalf for money, as happened in the first use of DNA mass screening in a murder investigation, to an individual giving a sample on behalf of a friend in the case of a paternity dispute.

It is also interesting to note in the context of substitution that it has been known for an alternative problem to arise, that is, a mother claiming that an individual is her offspring, but being ruled out as the mother. This may seem an unusual situation, but it has been known in cases of immigration disputes that attempts have been made to demonstrate that the individual requesting entry into a country claims an individual already resident as their mother. Such people are usually maternal aunts or other close relatives, but are still easily ruled out on the basis of DNA profiles. Maternity disputes are unusual outside this area, for the simple reasons that, while there are usually only two people present at the conception, there are frequently a lot more present at the birth, and during the months preceding birth a pregnancy is difficult, though not impossible, to hide. Samples of this type are usually blood, although as the technology increases in sophistication it is not necessary to use blood for DNA analysis, as other DNA-containing material is just as good. It is also possible for deliberate substitution of a sample to take place by a third party. This would be a very unusual situation, but it could potentially arise.

These errors involving a complete sample are theoretically straightforward to obviate. In cases where paternity disputes, maternity disputes or immigration claims are involved, it is only acceptable for an approved blood taker to take the sample. It is most unlikely that this individual will know the person from whom the sample is being taken, but if they did this would be seen as a conflict of interests. To make sure the court knows from which person the blood originated, photographs, usually two passport sized, are signed by the blood taker. It is not possible for the blood taker to be sure that the person providing the sample is who he says he is, but he can certify that the photograph is of that person. So sending along a friend or relative should not help the subterfuge, unless the two people look very similar indeed. In criminal cases the situation is partially reversed, since samples are taken while the accused is in custody, in which case there is usually little dispute that the person from whom the blood was taken is the same person who is in court. In both these situations samples, once taken, are put in tamper-proof bags which cannot be opened without damage to the seal. These are then passed to the testing laboratory, where the seals are checked before any work is carried out on the sample.

It can be readily appreciated that tampering with samples of this type will usually produce a negative result. In the case of samples originating from an unknown person, this is not necessarily so.

Samples originating from a crime scene which are to be used to prepare a DNA profile have to be handled with great care to avoid contamination. These sorts of samples can be any material containing DNA. These includes blood, saliva, semen, mucus, skin or hairs. Hairs are a special case, and will be dealt with in more detail below. Samples of this type do not have a recognised individual as their originator. It is the purpose of the sample to produce a profile which can be used to either exclude an individual as the originator, which is an inarguable result, or include an individual as the originator, which has an associated probability rather than a certainty.

With these types of sample it is imperative that they are not handled with ungloved hands, as this can add extraneous DNA which will make the eventual result confusing and possibly completely useless. Deliberate mixing of these samples would be difficult, though not impossible, as it would require the artificial introduction of DNA-containing material into a crime scene before samples are taken away. This would either be to incriminate an individual or to cast doubt on a person having been present at the scene. This also tells us something fundamental about DNA evidence: while it may be possible to prove to the satisfaction of a court that DNA was found at a scene, the assumption that it puts an individual at the scene cannot be proven by the DNA alone. Of course in some cases, such as rape, it is hard to argue otherwise, but when it is a cigarette end which has provided a DNA profile it is more difficult to be certain that the cigarette was smoked there without other evidence.

2.3.2 Accidental introduction of errors

Accidental introduction of errors to the sample generally take the form of contamination of a sample with extraneous DNA. One such way in which this might happen when blood is being collected is for a blood tube to be used which is incorrectly labelled. It would only be expected that this would happen in a crowded and busy department, and then very rarely.

Accidental contamination at a crime scene is possible, but less likely than accidental contamination within the testing laboratory. The very sensitive techniques now used in DNA analysis can easily result in the wrong DNA being analysed by mistake. This can happen simply by cross-contamination of one sample with another, but the precise point at which this takes place can be very difficult to determine.

Part of the problem with this type of contamination is that, once DNA has been extracted from cells and has been processed ready for analysis, it can be visualised almost like an infectious particle. Should this DNA get back into the system, it will be preferentially replicated and can completely mask the true result. By contrast, accidental contamination in the laboratory of samples before processing has started is easier to recognise.

Contamination by already processed DNA may only be detected by checking the result against other profiles. This procedure relies on the very low probability that two samples will produce the same profile. This is not impossible, of course, but if two samples do match then the samples can be rerun or, where possible, fresh samples can be obtained. If at this point it can be shown that contamination has taken place, an audit should be undertaken to ascertain, if possible, where the problem arose. In the case of accidental contamination taking place before or during processing the result is often seen as a mixed profile, interpreted as being DNA from at least two different individuals. In this case the profiles can be checked for the origin of the contamination, but mixed profiles can be a natural product of some samples, such as vaginal swabs in cases of rape. The methods of dealing with samples to obviate this problem before a DNA profile is produced will be described below. Other forms of accidental contamination can occur if a crime scene sample, like a cigarette, has been shared by two or more people.

Considerable effort is put into controlling problems of contamination within the testing laboratories, because it is recognised that accidental contamination is most likely to take place while samples are being processed. If control of this problem is not tackled at the time that the laboratory is set up, it can be extremely difficult to put right afterwards.

Systems which should be in place at the time that work commences include:

- all glassware should be washed and rinsed in distilled water;
- all solutions are sterilised to breakdown extraneous DNA;
- all plastic disposables should be sterilised before use and used only once;
- handling of any container or reagent should only be carried out while wearing gloves;
- solutions should be stored at a temperature which slows degradation;
- all reagents should be recorded with batch numbers and date received;
- all reagents should be clearly labelled with reagent name, use by date, or date made up, and kept in suitable storage conditions.

It is also important that sample reception, processing, and results generation are carried out in different suites of rooms, so that sample flow is in one direction only, from reception through DNA extraction, replication of DNA, to finally producing a reportable result. This also extends to limiting protective clothing, gloves and laboratory coats to one particular area. This should stop any contamination being moved from one part of the laboratory to another.

2.3.3 Naturally occurring errors

Some errors associated with a sample are unavoidable and quite normal. These are samples originating from one individual, but with DNA from two people present. The most obvious situation of this sort would be in the case of rape, where an intimate swab would be expected to yield cells from the assaulted and cells, usually as sperm, from the attacker. Cases such as these are sufficiently well known for systems to be in place to sort out the problem. The solution is based on the robust nature of sperm cells.

In cases where vaginal swabs have been taken and microscopical assessment of the sample suggests the presence of sperm heads, a differential extraction can be attempted. When sperm heads are seen to be present in a sample it does not mean that there are not other cells also present. Indeed, it is reasonable to assume that there will also be epithelial cells present, some possibly in the semen, but most from the vaginal wall. Being a mucus membrane, cell loss is continuous and would be on the swab with the semen. Sperm cells are physically resilient, far more so than epithelial cells, so treating the sample with disruptive solutions which disrupt epithelial cells, but not sperm cells, results in epithelial DNA in solution along with intact sperm cells. Spinning this cocktail at very high speed in a centrifuge results in the sperm cells precipitating while the epithelial DNA remains in solution. Further sample preparation can then be carried out on the sperm heads alone and the epithelial DNA already in solution. Using this technique, it is possible to produce DNA profiles which do not contain mixtures of DNA.

Other naturally occurring mixtures of DNA in samples can arise from the site from which the sample was taken. If a kitchen knife was suspected of having been used in an attack and had blood on it, there would be a number of possible sources of DNA that could be found. It could be human blood, it could be blood from more than one human, it could be animal blood, or it could be a mixture of both human and animal blood. Under these circumstances, if the background research has been carried out adequately it is not necessary to directly address these questions, as a DNA profile should only be produced from human material.

This brings us to a very important point. When sections of DNA are being investigated for their potential use in forensic applications, the sequences must be unique to humans. They may be embedded within genes which are found widely throughout the animal kingdom, but the precise areas used to produce a DNA profile must be human-specific. Of course, it would be impossible to test every mammal to see if they would produce a DNA profile, and reason indicates that this is unnecessary, but it is important to check that commensal species, like rats and mice and food species, do not produce a profile in their own right or interfere with the production of a profile from human DNA when the two are mixed. Extensive work is carried out on those species which are likely to leave DNA traces, so that any mixture between human and animal DNA can be ignored without the risk of a result being generated which would only serve to confuse or invalidate the results.

2.4 Sample degradation

The longer biological material spends unprotected in the environment the more it breaks down. This process of decay depends for its speed on several factors, such as temperature, humidity, presence of micro-organisms such as bacteria and fungi, and insects, many of which use such material as a food supply for their larvae. As far as samples for DNA profiling are concerned, the less decay the better. When DNA profiling was originally introduced, it required quite substantial sections of DNA to be available, with no breaks or damage caused by decay. This was not always possible to find because DNA, like all organic molecules, is quickly recycled back into the environment if it is unprotected. Breakdown tends to start at random down the length of the molecule, so the shorter the piece of DNA needed for profiling, the more likely it is that one will be found intact. Current methods of profiling use much shorter sections of DNA, which consequently survive longer in adverse conditions before they are all broken down beyond use, but even here there are limits after which it is simply not possible to produce a profile of DNA from the cell nucleus. There is, however, an alternative source of DNA which can sometimes be used, although it has lower discriminatory power and also has some distinct limitations. This is mitochondrial DNA (mtDNA), not found in the cell nucleus but in cellular organelles called mitochondria. Mitochondria are the enzyme powerhouses of the cell where metabolic activity comes from and energy is produced. Mitochondria have a major advantage in forensic studies in that they are found in all cells, but also in hair shafts, where no nuclear DNA is found, as well as inside bone and teeth. This puts them inside some of the most well protected areas of the body, areas which are among the very last to succumb to decay. So even when all normal attempts to produce a DNA profile have failed, mitochondrial DNA can sometimes be put to use instead. The methods and limitations of mitochondrial DNA (mtDNA) analysis will be dealt with in Chapter 5, as they are distinct from nuclear DNA.

In the future it is likely that single nucleotide polymorphisms (SNP) analysis will become either an additional method in forensic DNA analysis, or a method which will replace the current systems entirely. With the need to construct databases for comparison, replacing the current system would require replacing the national database as well, which would involve a great deal of time and money. Although SNP analysis uses a very much smaller change in DNA than the current systems of short tandem repeat (STR) analysis, which uses the number of repeats in a sequence, the initial requirements of a sample are not much different from STR analysis. The result of this is that SNP analysis is only very slightly less sensitive to sample degradation than the current STR analysis. This is a limit of technology rather than science, so until new methods of analysing DNA are available, the limits of resolution in DNA analysis have been reached and are determined by the degree to which sample degradation has taken place.

2.5 Sample confusion: a forensic perspective

It is possible to cause a real difference to the outcome of an analysis by creating an alternative sample. Not only is this easy to carry out, but it has the added difficulty of it being very difficult to know when it has taken place with some types of sample. Confusion would be unlikely in cases of assault, where large bloodstains are available, or in cases of rape, in which a differential extraction is carried out.

Older techniques of DNA analysis, which used relatively large amounts of DNA to produce a result, had one significant advantage over current and future techniques. It was relatively difficult to deliberately confuse an analysis on the part of a criminal by artificially introducing a DNA sample; to do so would require considerable forethought and a relatively large sample. This is not so with current and future methods. The manner in which DNA analysis is currently carried out is by 'targeting' very specific small areas of the entire genome. It would be very simple for an educated criminal to produce a spray of all the different profiles so that it would be impossible to determine which belonged to the perpetrator. Although this would initially seem to be far-fetched, it would in fact be very simple to carry out and the result would be the same as a criminal leaving thousands of different fingerprints at the scene of a crime to confuse the police, or by careful planting, incriminate a known individual. The original methods of DNA profiling required such large amounts of DNA for analysis that this sort of action would not be feasible – it would need such large quantities of DNA containing material that a subterfuge of this nature would be essentially impossible. At this point the most important aspect of the analysis is that DNA is artificially amplified, and this is why such small samples can be used. This is both its strength and its weakness. Such small samples are useable that it becomes relatively easy to deposit at a burglary something as apparently innocuous as a cigarette end smoked by another person. DNA profiles produced from such a sample would not then match the profile of the accused, unless, of course, the accused was innocent and someone wanted to deliberately incriminate him or her.

It is also true that once a sample has been through the process of extraction and amplification, contamination of other samples by the product is a very real problem. This is not just because it would create the appearance of a mixture, but because if amplification products are mixed with DNA which has not been amplified, it is the amplification products which are preferentially used in the chemical reaction. This situation could be exploited by an unscrupulous individual at a crime scene. Using a solution of DNA containing already amplified DNA to mask any DNA accidentally deposited, it would be impossible to sort out the true situation using DNA analysis.

From these two possibilities we can see that, as in the case of cigarette ends, DNA may be able to tell us who might have been in contact with an item, but not where. Also, DNA on its own may not necessarily be conclusive, and all the evidence should be considered. There is nothing wrong in combining evidence, so long as the evidence which is combined is independent, but it is important that we do not become obsessed with applying numerical values to probabilities and possibilities. As we shall see in Chapters 5 and 6, numerical data has to be dealt with in a very cautious way if the audience, in this case the court, is not going to become lost and confused.

SUMMARY

Samples for DNA profiling should be as complete as possible, and as free from decay and degradation as is practicable. This is not always how samples are received, so the handling and methods used to process a sample will have considerable bearing on the outcome of any tests carried out. Even damaged DNA can yield a useful result if handled correctly. It is of paramount importance when carrying out DNA analysis in a forensic situation that the sample is treated with the utmost care. The extreme sensitivity of current techniques of DNA analysis can result in any number of problems. The chain of custody of a sample and its precise origins, so far as are known, must be recorded. Transport of samples in anything but a tamper-proof bag, that is, one which cannot be undone without permanently damaging the seal, should not be accepted.

The generation of errors has to be controlled as much as possible. Some types of contamination can be virtually eliminated by careful laboratory work, but deliberate contamination can only be controlled with detailed rules covering the chain of custody of samples from collection through to analysis.

CHAPTER 3

BLOOD GROUPS AND OTHER CELLULAR MARKERS

INTRODUCTION

Perhaps the most widely known test of biological material is blood grouping. It is not generally thought that blood grouping represents a form of DNA analysis, but this is precisely what it is. We can justify this by remembering that blood groups are determined by inheritance of genes and, therefore, if we determine a blood group we can also learn something about the individual's genetic make-up.

Although blood grouping has been used as the basis for some systems of personal identification, it is something of a blunt instrument. For example, it is quite straightforward when interpreting a blood grouping test to tell whether the blood sample matches that of an individual who has been typed for comparison. If the sample and the person do not match, it is clear and unequivocal that the blood did not come from that person. If there is a match, however, the converse is not true. The range of possibilities is relatively small, so even the unusual blood groups are well represented in a population.

The traditional, and first, use of blood grouping was in paternity disputes. Under these circumstances, exactly the same inference can be drawn from a test. It is possible to exclude paternity, but not possible to be sure about an inclusion, other than producing a probability figure on which the court has to make a judgment as to whether it is of any significance to the case being heard.

Historically, this difficulty of interpreting such low level data has caused some problems for the courts. In the US, during the middle of the 20th century, blood test evidence was viewed in a variety of ways, as given by a few examples:

- 1956, *Jordan v Davis* (1989) 339 Nature 501–05, Maine. Blood tests are admissible when non-paternity is indicated.
- 1957, Wisconsin. Blood tests are admissible, but with consideration of the other evidence.

- 1959, New York. Demonstration of non-paternity is conclusive evidence.
- 1963, *Beck v Beck* (1989) 339 Nature 501–05, Colorado. Blood tests are admissible as evidence for the defence when they demonstrate non-paternity.

Perhaps surprisingly, during this period there were cases in which paternity was excluded and yet settlement out of court was deemed the best option by the excluded father.

It is now possible to use a range of different blood groups for personal identification; it is not just the well known ABO system and rhesus factors which can be used. When blood groupings are used in forensic cases a relatively large sample is required, but it does have the advantage of currently being both cheap and quick. Large scale pre-screens are possible using blood groups, which would otherwise be both prohibitively expensive and time consuming if they went directly for DNA testing, even though the unit cost has reduced considerably in the last few years.

In general, the method of blood typing is based on the antibody/antigen reaction. To see how these systems can be used in forensic applications it is worth considering the way in which the system works. Whenever a foreign substance is injected into an organism with an immune system, like you or I, the body takes action to control what might be toxic material. The foreign material is the antigen, and the body's reaction is to produce antibodies to that antigen. Antibodies tend to be highly specific to antigens, although cross-reactions do sometimes occur.

By taking advantage of this process, it has become possible to artificially manipulate the system to our advantage and thereby prevent many infectious diseases. If a section of an infectious organism is used as the antigen, or possibly the entire, but killed, organism, the body produces antibodies which are ready and able to stop the infection from taking hold should an individual come into contact with the live disease. This is the basis of vaccination, to help our immune system against invading organisms which could kill us before antibodies could be produced. Although vaccination is not always as efficacious as we would like, there is one species which, being incapable of life without its host, was wiped out as a wild species in 1979 by vaccination: smallpox (which, incidentally, gave us the word 'vaccination' from the biological name for it: *vaccinia*). It is, however, interesting to note that in evolutionary terms our immunological system, which is not only responsible for our response to invading organisms but also the cause of such irritations as hayfever and asthma, probably originated for a completely different reason. Consider the statistics of a large, long lived organism such as a human. We have approximately 100,000,000 cells in every gram of tissue, and every time a cell divides it risks a mutation at the rate of about one in 100,000 to one in 100,000,000. So we have lots of cells risking mutations every time they divide. One of the mutations we definitely do not want is that which results in cancer. It is the ability of the body to recognise these unwanted and dangerous mutations that allow us to be so large, long lived and complex.

3.1 ABO blood groups

With blood groups the process is slightly different because, unlike acquired immunity, blood groups represent natural antibodies that do not require antigens to be present for their expression. The term used for these antibodies is 'acquired'. Acquired antibodies are required by the body for some reason, or sometimes just appear to be present for, as yet, no discernible reason. When incompatible blood types are mixed, the blood cells agglutinate by reaction to the antibodies in the serum. This is because the red blood cells carry antigens. The name of a person's blood group derives from the antigens on the blood cell surface. It is evident that individuals with a particular antigen cannot have the corresponding antibody or their own blood would clot. The four major ABO blood groups and their attendant properties are listed below:

BLOOD GROUP	BLOOD CELL ANTIGEN	BLOOD SERUM ANTIBODY
A	A	anti-B
B	B	anti-A
AB	A and B	none
O	none	anti-A and anti-B

Broadly, this means that when blood transfusions are being considered it is important to have as close a match as possible if whole blood is being used, but if cell free serum is used group O can receive serum from O, A, B and AB;

group B can receive serum from B and AB; group A can receive serum from A and AB; but people of blood group AB can only receive transfusions from other AB donors.

3.2 Rhesus blood groups

Another well known blood group of medical importance is the rhesus (Rh) factor. This system takes its name from rhesus monkeys, which were used as donors of blood used to immunise rabbits. When serum from these rabbits was tested on human samples in New York, it was discovered that 85% of the population were Rh positive, that is, the serum agglutinated their blood cells. This study was stimulated by an important observation that occasionally infants were born suffering from a characteristic form of anaemia. The nature of the disease is a case of acquired immunity associated with blood groups. It arises when an Rh negative mother has an Rh positive child: blood passage across the placenta, especially during birth, generates anti-Rh antibodies. These cause anaemia in later pregnancies by destroying the foetal red blood cells. Interestingly, although there are only two phenotypes – expression of the rhesus factor as either Rh positive or Rh negative – the number of alleles is far greater, so there are many routes by which rhesus factors can be inherited. Consequently, although Rh factors have a very low forensic potential, looking at the genotype – the genes which generate the Rh factors – is much more informative. Because Rh factors are inherited quite independently of other blood groups, the data can be combined from several results generated from different blood groups for use in forensic applications. Some of these other grouping systems are described below.

3.3 MN blood groups

Another system of blood groups, independent of both the ABO and rhesus factors, are the MN blood groups. The method by which these are inherited is by far the most straightforward of the three systems described here. MN blood groups are associated with acquired antibodies. There are two varieties of gene, or allele, found, one of which is called M and the other N. Because neither of these is dominant over the other, there are three possible outcomes: M, N and MN. Again, being inherited independently of other blood groups, the data for MN systems can be combined to increase the evidential value of blood groups. Even so, because they tend to have relatively complicated modes of inheritance, the MN system being an exception to this, it can be quite difficult to combine data to produce probabilities.

The above three examples of blood groups give an indication of the range of systems which can be found. Before looking in detail at the way that blood groups are used in a forensic context, it would be instructive to look at the range of other blood groups which are available for analysis besides the three blood grouping systems described above.

3.4 The range of inherited blood groups

As the ABO blood groups were the first to be clearly worked out, they are referred to as 'classical' blood groups. Altogether, there are approximately 15 different known blood groups in humans. For the most part, they are not generally very informative in forensic applications, but do serve valuable biological functions. In some cases they are of value in tissue typing, where having an exact match is more important than with blood transfusions. Some of the different systems include Lewis, Diego, Lutheran, PGM, Kell and Kidd. Some of these are inherited in such a complicated way, and are tested by using very specialised techniques, that they are of little use in forensic applications.

3.5 How blood groups are inherited

All blood groups are inherited genetically. This may appear self-evident, but not all inherited factors are genetic. In the case of blood groups the method of inheritance is quite well understood, but it is slightly more complicated than some more straightforward genetic traits, such as cystic fibrosis or sickle cell anaemia, which are both single gene defects with a very clear method of inheritance. Not all genetic diseases are inherited in such a clear fashion as these two examples, and neither are blood groups. Blood group inheritance is complicated because, unlike the simple systems which are of an either/or type – that is, you either have Rh positive or Rh negative, you cannot have both – blood groups are inherited in a range of ways, some of which are simpler than others.

This apparent complexity arises not simply because there is more than one type in a blood group system, as in the ABO blood groups, but also because there can be several ways to inherit even an apparently simple two-blood-type system such as the rhesus factor. An important starting point in the explanation of this is that we all have two copies of every gene on every chromosome, except the genes found on sex chromosomes. For the purposes of forensic applications, it currently remains the case that all tested systems are present as two copies. One of the copies is inherited from the father and one from the mother, but – and it is a big but – there may be several different versions scattered through the population. So although an individual will express a specific blood group, there may be several different ways in which this may be achieved.

One of the simplest systems for blood group inheritance is that found in the MN system. Although it is of use in forensic applications, giving an additional piece of information which can be used in probability calculations, the MN blood group is of no practical value for blood transfusions. From the very first recognition of the system it was obviously controlled by only two alleles, or different gene types, which would have originated as one from the mother and one from the father. But because the carriers of these genes can be either blood type M (where both genes are the same), N (also where both genes are the same), or MN (where the two genes are different), it was also realised that this exhibits codominance. While we are all aware of dominant and recessive traits such as colour blindness, in truth most inherited characteristics are inherited in a more complicated manner. So codominance is effectively seen as the blending of characters, so anathema of straightforward Mendelian genetics where traits are inherited as distinct entities, with one being dominant over the other. Just as the flowers of a cross between red and white snapdragons will only produce pink flowers, as humans we are neither black nor white, but a blend of all manner of mixed genes working together. As we shall see later, the interpretation for geneticists of codominance of more than two genes can become really quite intricate, and may in the near future become a legally contentious issue, with insurance companies wanting to use information about genetic make-up in assessing risks even though few professional geneticists would even try such a calculation, and insurance companies do not have the expertise for solving such difficult conundrums in the first place.

3.5.1 MN blood grouping

In the example of codominance in MN blood groups, this means that if both parents are homozygous for M – that is, being type M and having both copies of the gene as M – all the children will be M, and likewise, with N type parents all the children will be N. But if one parent is M and the other N, all the children will have received one M gene and one N gene, so will be MN – that is, heterozygous – having two different genes and expressing them both. So, in the case of both parents being MN, the options are for the children to be either type M – having received an M allele from both parents; type N – having received an N allele from both parents; or MN – where they receive an M from one parent and an N from the other. Most individuals are unaware of their MN type, as it has little or no medical significance, but population studies have shown that the M and N genes are present in the population as approximately 50% each. This was worked out long before the gene itself had been localised; it was done simply by the traditional means of looking at the ratios of the blood types. In this case, it was easily shown that M types and N types were found in equal numbers, while MN blood types were present in double the numbers.

Intimately associated with the MN blood group is another pair of antigens: designated S and s. MN and Ss are referred to as linked: they are separate genes but are so close together that in any given family inheritance of one form will automatically imply inheritance of the other. The value of this is that it adds a little more information in paternity cases, although it should be remembered that being separate genes does mean that occasionally they will be inherited independently. The reason they will not particularly aid in paternity cases is because this linkage would suggest that if you were to test the MN group you would be able to make a good prediction as to the Ss group, and vice versa. It is a bit like saying that it is of little help in identifying a bicycle by saying it has pedals: bicycles and pedals are linked.

3.5.2 Rhesus (Rh)

Rhesus factors, so important in producing successful blood transfusions, are inherited in a very straightforward manner but, unlike the previous example of MN blood groups, rhesus exhibits a system of completely dominant and recessive expression. Rh positive phenotypes are dominant over Rh negative. The gene alleles of the rhesus system come in three different types so closely linked together that they are inherited as a block. The presence of even a single dominant allele in any of these three genes results in an Rh positive phenotype. Because of this weighting against the inheritance of a complete set of recessive alleles, the Rh negative phenotype is relatively rare. There is also something of particular interest in the level of this rarity in that it varies from ethnic group to ethnic group. So, for example, a large study in Sweden showed that approximately 85% of those tested were Rh positive and 15% were Rh negative. Smaller studies in the US came out with a similar figure for white Americans, but black Americans were about 90% Rh positive and 10% Rh negative. An even more extreme variation was found among native American Indians from Oklahoma, where 99% were Rh positive and only 1% Rh negative. The comparison between white Americans and Swedes is as would be expected, since white Americans would have mostly originated from Europe.

3.5.3 ABO blood groups

Inheritance of ABO blood groups seems simple enough, but interpreting the results in families can be quite difficult. Large scale studies have shown that blood group A children only arise if one of the two parents is also either group A or group AB. Similarly, B individuals require a parent who is also B or AB. We can say from this that the alleles causing the blood groups have a hierarchy of dominance: A and B are codominant, that is, the genes are expressed whenever they are present, but the allele which results in blood group O is recessive to both of them. Put another way, if alleles are present for both A and O the blood group is A; when alleles for both B and O are present the result is blood group B; presence of alleles for both A and B give blood group AB, but when the only alleles present are both O, then the blood group is O. The picture is a little more complicated in practice, as it is possible to determine the presence of several different versions of the A alleles, varying in quite minor ways and not generally of any importance.

3.6 Forensic applications of blood groups

The most important primary attribute of all tests of trace materials, whether biological or not, is that they can exclude an individual completely from being the depositor of the crime sample. What they most definitely cannot do is make a categorical statement that a specified individual was the originator of the tested material. This is a very important point to note and, as we will see later, it has a significant bearing on the interpretation that a jury makes of evidence, depending on the manner in which it is expressed.

Blood group analysis is indirect analysis of DNA, DNA making up the genes which are expressed as blood groups. It can be surmised, therefore, that since we are working one step away from the genes themselves, variation in the form of mutations will be much reduced. Inherent within DNA is an ability to cope with mutations, which as we have seen can occur quite commonly, without this affecting the final gene product, in this case blood groups. It is perhaps interesting to note that although blood groups are generated by DNA and genes, when testing clotting of red blood cells the test is carried out on the only cells in the body which do not themselves contain a nucleus or DNA. This testing at a distance has one considerable advantage. When blood transfusions take place it is usually only necessary to check the ABO and rhesus blood groups to avoid problems of clotting, so when an ABO/Rh blood test is used in a forensic investigation after a blood transfusion, it may test the donor's blood, but as this has to be the same as the recipient's and will be cleared from the system relatively quickly anyway, it will make no difference to the result. This is also true of cases of bone marrow transplants which take place in some cases of leukaemia, but leukaemia can cause problems when looking at ABO/Rh blood groups as expression of these can be modified by this condition.

Although this traditional blood testing process can be seen as a relatively blunt forensic instrument compared with direct DNA analysis, it does have the advantage of reliability. With direct analysis of DNA this claim cannot always be met. Although it would seem that if we tested for a blood group we would expect to find the same result as testing for sequencing a gene for a blood group, this is simply not so. In the case of an individual having had a bone marrow transplant, the DNA sequences which are used for comparison will be different from the simple analysis of the blood groups. This problem will be explored further in Chapter 4, dealing with all forms of direct DNA analysis.

Given that there are only four possible variants of the ABO blood types, which are A, B, AB and O, regardless of the underlying genetic basis, this gives us four blood group types. The rhesus (Rh) system only gives us two alternatives, but since they are inherited on different chromosomes, or sections of DNA, to the ABO system, this blood type can be regarded as being inherited separately from the ABO system. So with four ABO blood groups and two Rh groups, it is only possible to recognise a maximum of eight different types: simply 2 Rh groups x 4 ABO groups = 8. But this simple analysis may not tell us all that is significant about a blood group analysis. The complexity and evidential significance increases because we are not looking at a straightforward one in eight chance of finding a similar result: as we have seen, the various blood groups are represented at different frequencies, so the value of any given result can be quite different depending upon the group, or proposed group, from which a sample originated.

We can take as broadly accurate the figures for blood group frequencies as follows in western European populations, remembering that some small and isolated populations may have marginally different frequencies:

A	42%
B	9%
AB	3%
O	46%

It has also been reported that some Asian populations have a frequency of blood group B of around 36%. This difference is probably of some biological significance as a result of evolutionary pressure. An example of this sort of advantage can be found in the case of sickle cell anaemia. This condition is inherited in a dominant and recessive manner and the underlying biochemical problem is now well understood.

Individuals with sickle cell anaemia have red blood cells with abnormal haemoglobin, which results in them collapsing into a characteristic shape like a sickle. Unfortunately these red blood cells then tend to clog the smaller capillaries, which causes the severe problems associated with this condition. Inheritance of sickle cell anaemia is recessive, so only individuals carrying both genes, one from the father and one from the mother, will have the condition, although carriers, that is, individuals with one normal gene and one sickling gene, do exhibit problems during oxygen stress such as high altitude or severe exercise. It should be realised that this, like so many similar conditions, is not a gene for a disease so much as a variant of a normal gene which works in a different way. Population studies indicated quite quickly that sickle cell anaemia was almost exclusively associated with equatorial Africa, with a few other notable sites on other continents. Since sickle cell anaemia is so debilitating, often leading to an early death, the question to be asked is why has the gene been maintained in the population? The answer to this seems to be that the carriers, those with only a single copy of the gene and therefore not exhibiting symptoms under normal conditions, are less susceptible to malaria. So although the disease kills, carriers are, in evolutionary terms, fitter than normal individuals.

So we can see that some blood groups are more likely to be found than others, which can have a significant affect on the weight which is given to the interpretation of the result. Because rhesus groups are inherited independently of ABO blood groups, the probabilities can be combined. The construction of a probability and the manner in which it is normally expressed will be dealt with in more detail in Chapter 5, covering statistical analysis of both simple blood group tests and DNA tests.

When evidence is presented of a scientific nature it is frequently expected, and most often presented, in numerical form. The trend here is to always present the data in the same way, but it can be easily recognised that this may not always be the best way. For example, the frequency of blood group A is about 42%, and this is much easier to understand than one in 2.4 for the simple reason that, quite rightly, 0.4 of a person is not a sensible value to use.

With the number of blood groups available where the mode of inheritance has been worked out along with the population frequencies it should be relatively easy to determine paternity, although in criminal cases the issues are sufficiently different to render blood typing in most cases a very blunt instrument. This is because to produce a comprehensive and believable result would require more blood of an acceptable quality than is normally available at a crime scene. It is possible to determine the blood groups of mummies that are in a suitable state of preservation, but it is important that the body is preserved, as blood group antigens are highly susceptible to bacterial and fungal decay. This can take place quite quickly under the right conditions, such as somewhere warm and damp, in fact anywhere that you would consider suitable for food spoilage!

Some of the earliest and most profound uses of blood grouping in a forensic context were in paternity disputes. Given access to a sufficiently large sample, most questions of paternity can be resolved using blood group analysis, but may require the use of quite a large range of blood groups. Exactly what the reason for this is remains a biological conundrum, since for the most part blood groups have no outward affect. It has been noted that in some cases where a woman does not know which of two partners is the father of her child, there is an unexpectedly large similarity in the various blood groups between the two putative fathers, requiring rather more blood types to be investigated than would normally be the case.

The problem here is an extension of the normal situation in paternity disputes. If two fathers have the same blood group it is not possible to say which one is the father. It can be appreciated here that it is not necessary to know anything about the frequency of the different blood types in a population, since all that is required is a determination of whether a specified individual is or is not the father. This only holds true when it is a case of named alternative fathers, that is, in the simplest situation, of a choice of two fathers. Under these circumstances, blood grouping is carried out until one of the two alternatives is excluded from being the father, at which point the named alternative is ruled as the father.

The process of exclusion of an individual is the most powerful aspect of blood grouping, as it renders the only absolute statement that can be made using biological evidence. So although it is possible to say that an individual cannot be the father, it is never possible to say that an individual is the father, but only that there is a probability of him being so. This becomes a contentious issue when there is no named alternative father, in that inclusion does require some knowledge of the frequencies at which the various forms of the tested blood groups are to be found in the relevant population. As we have seen above, there is little relevance in claiming an inclusion of a suggested father on the basis of a single test of rhesus factors, resulting in the information that the father must be Rh positive, when approximately 85% of the population is Rh positive. A complete denial when faced with this sort of information must be taken seriously. It is for this reason that databases have to be constructed of the various alleles which are going to be encountered.

It may be thought that frequency databases all contain very similar, if not identical, information. This is not true, as the information held within a database of gene frequencies extends far beyond a simple value of probability, and such information should be treated with a great deal of care. As we shall see in Chapter 6, covering database construction and use, the intrinsic value of such a database may be tarnished by potential uses. However, generating anonymous blood group analysis data is different, since it gives a clear understanding of the probability of finding any given blood group combination by chance alone, without the associated problems of human rights.

It should be realised that it is now very rare for blood grouping to be used on a widespread basis for paternity disputes, but this is not because direct DNA analysis is necessarily a more powerful tool. An exclusion on a blood group is still an exclusion and just as definite, but an inclusion could be argued over because of the number of other people that could carry the same blood groups and could be responsible for the pregnancy. Similarly, parental disputes, although rare, can be readily solved using traditional blood grouping. These are the unusual cases where there has been, or thought to have been, a mistake in the labelling of offspring in a maternity unit such that two sets of parents are disputing two different children. The easiest way of demonstrating the way in which blood grouping can be used in these sorts of situations is to use a number of hypothetical examples.

In the case of two families who suspect that an incorrect labelling on a maternity ward has resulted in taking home the wrong child, the analysis is simple because we are dealing with a genetically closed unit: that is, all the protagonists agree that they are related, it is just the relationship between individuals which is in dispute and therefore is to be tested. In cases such as these, blood grouping tests have potentially major advantages and disadvantages over other systems such as direct DNA testing.

Major advantages are that a clear result does not have to be justified by probabilities; a blood group test which rules out one couple as the parents, while not excluding the other couple, gives a clear indication of parentage. This is shown in the example below:

PARENTAL BLOOD GROUPS ON THE ABO SYSTEM		BLOOD GROUP OF CHILD
Mother: A	Father: AB	O
Mother: O	Father: O	B

Here we have a clear result: parents who are A/AB cannot produce a child with blood group O, so a switch has taken place. But note that such a conclusion is only a result of this being a closed system: there is no suggestion of any other person being involved, so a clear result is produced. Even so, this is still a potentially flawed technique given different combinations of ABO blood groups. For example:

PARENTAL BLOOD GROUPS ON THE ABO SYSTEM		BLOOD GROUP OF CHILD
Mother: A	Father: B	O
Mother: O	Father: O	O

No information is available from this analysis because both sets of parents could produce a child of blood group O. It would be necessary to use additional blood group analysis to solve this conundrum.

In disputes of paternity where a mother claims an individual is the father of her child, blood groups can be used as a means of ruling out an individual, that is, producing an exclusion, quite effectively, but are poor includers and should be used with great care, if at all, in paternity disputes. The problem arises because there are normally only two people present at conception, so relying on a single piece of low discrimination evidence is unwise. Adding in progressively more blood groups will increase the likelihood, but it is never going to be possible to be as certain about paternity as with DNA analysis.

These constraints also hold true for blood grouping used in criminal cases. As we have seen, blood testing has been used as a preliminary screen prior to more detailed DNA analysis. This was carried out using ABO blood groups and another blood group system called PGM, which took place in Leicestershire in 1987, but it is less likely to be done in that way now as both the speed and cost of DNA profiling has come down considerably since then. Pre-screening was used because at that time DNA profiling was specialised, time consuming and expensive, requiring as it did a lot of highly skilled staff. With the extensive automation of laboratories and the economies of scale now available, it can be both quicker and cheaper to use DNA profiling directly. This is especially true when other ancillary factors are considered, such as the time and equipment needed to take a liquid blood sample from an individual rather than mouth swabs or plucked hair, which can be used for DNA analysis. Besides these factors a major cost is manpower. When forensic profiling started, the scientists carrying it out were highly skilled, having to understand exactly what they were doing, and consequently it was a very expensive activity to carry out. Like many breakthrough processes, time has allowed development of methods and recipes which can be followed quite easily to produce a reliable result.

SUMMARY

Blood groups have a long history and are effectively testing DNA one step removed. DNA in the form of genes is code for the blood groups, so testing blood groups tells us something about the genes. As there are usually several different forms of a gene which will result in the same blood group, testing the blood group will not necessarily tell us which form of the gene is present. This means that there is a smaller range of blood groups than genes, so blood grouping has many disadvantages. However, any exclusion using blood groups, whether it is in a paternity dispute or a mismatch between the blood of an assailant found on a victim and the accused, are all exclusions as powerful as any produced using a DNA profile. If an inclusion is found under the same circumstances, the limitations of blood groups becomes more obvious. Their very low individual discriminatory power results in several tests being done and still only resulting in relatively small probabilities when compared to DNA profiling.

Although blood grouping is relatively cheap and quick, this is rapidly being caught up with by DNA profiling. It must also be remembered that the mode of inheritance of some of these blood types is sufficiently complicated for us to question whether, even though an inclusion has been found, it is a real inclusion. The same blood groups can originate in a number of different ways, depending upon the individual's genetic make-up.

CHAPTER 4

DNA ANALYSIS

INTRODUCTION

Although DNA is seen as the ultimate analytical technique, the tools with which it is carried out and the nature of the results will change with time as techniques become more sophisticated. Indeed, this has already happened in the short space of time in which it has been used, and it has become a forensic tool of enormous power. DNA analysis has virtually replaced all other methods of trace analysis involving biological fluids. This is primarily due to it being possible to carry out DNA analysis on samples of a very small size and on virtually any type of biological material. Although blood groups can sometimes be produced from semen and other biological material, it cannot be carried out on the range of material that DNA will produce a result from.

The greatest advantage of DNA analysis also contains its greatest risk of error – that is, the sensitivity of the test. This sensitivity has extended the range of material which can be used for DNA analysis, which is especially significant in criminal cases, but it has repercussions for paternity testing as well. By being able to test such items as cigarette ends and the residual cells left when an envelope or stamp has been licked, hate mail and fraud have come under the umbrella of DNA testing. Not only has DNA analysis become more sensitive by orders of magnitude over the last decade, but it has also become concomitantly more reliable. It is quite likely that in the near future traditional fingerprinting will become virtually redundant, with DNA being extracted and analysed from fingerprints found on sound, clean surfaces being used as a substrate for DNA profiling. This is a technique which was successfully carried out experimentally by me in 1990. As we shall see, to reinforce the reliability of this sort of analysis it has become necessary to increase the control of the systems which are in place within testing laboratories to ensure the quality of results. In many cases it has been necessary to increase quality systems, and yet still errors can arise. This has resulted in an unprecedented level of standardisation between laboratories so that comparison can be made between results from different laboratories, not only within a single country, but also across international boundaries.

Stringent requirements are needed to successfully transfer a research tool into a routine laboratory of any type, whether this is a diagnostic or forensic laboratory. Without these detailed standardisation procedures the results are worse than useless – they are misleading. So the most important thing for the forensic scientist to remember is that quality is paramount; without it his or her result will be challenged in court. Similarly, DNA analysis has the potential to be very fast indeed, needing not days but only hours to complete an analysis. This is a considerable change from the first analyses, which could take weeks to complete.

Change has been the watch word for many years in forensic analysis of DNA, with each system being incompatible with the last. It was sometimes found that between conviction and appeal, the method of analysis had changed. There have been cases which have been brought to completion years after the crime was committed by using stored material which has eventually become viable for analysis, not due to changes in the sample, but to changes in the technology for treating the sample. This situation has slowed down somewhat with the construction of large scale databases, which are used for comparison between samples taken from individuals picked up for some reason, and material from crime scenes for which there is no known perpetrator. These databases are also used to compare scene of crime samples with named individuals who have already been in trouble and had samples taken. This may have been for completely unrelated crimes. With widespread use and increasing dependency on these databases for investigation of all manner of crimes, it has become more difficult to replace the currently used techniques. Even if a better system became available, and one most certainly will at some point, to change over completely from the current systems would be a huge task. Retesting the millions of samples would have such implications in terms of man hours and money that the new database would have to exist alongside the old database, probably for several years, while new data was collected.

In this chapter we will also introduce the topic of mitochondrial DNA (mtDNA), which is inherited in a quite different way to nuclear DNA.

Although not extensively used in forensic applications, it does have applications for which it is far better suited than any other form of DNA for analysis.

One thing that has happened during the last few years which causes some difficulty, even to researchers in the area, is jargon. A great deal of sloppy nomenclature has been, and still is, used when it comes to DNA profiling. It will be the intention that all terms will be explained in the text and the glossary, with a view to unifying the way in which these words are used, so that there is no confusion when details of a DNA profile are discussed in court. Research in the US has shown that the language used in court was sometimes not only misunderstood, but the very meaning of the words was not known. Under these circumstances, jargon should be avoided as much as possible. This is a common problem as language moves on, while institutionalised groups retain old words and meanings. An example of this change in public understanding may or may not be apocryphal, but it demonstrates the point. It was said that road signs at junctions were changed from 'HALT' to 'STOP' because an increasing number of people were unclear exactly what 'HALT' actually meant. In a similar way, as science moves forward new words are coined which have little or no meaning outside the science in which they were spawned, and it is incumbent on the scientist to try and avoid these words and terms as much as possible if the audience is going to understand what he or she is saying.

4.1 Why the structure and function of DNA is so useful in forensic applications

DNA is chemically a very simple molecule made up of four basic building blocks. It is because it is so simple that we have approximately 3,000,000,000 of these building blocks to generate the variety needed to code for the approximately 35,000–40,000 genes which make up a human genome. Because it is so simple it can be made in a laboratory, not just extracted from cells, but chemically constructed to a formula. So if we know the sequence of bases in a gene, we can generate an exact artificial copy. Of course, if the gene is very large constructing one artificially becomes increasingly difficult. This is because as the DNA replicates during cell division it has all manner of mechanisms to make sure it is a good and exact copy, which are not currently available in laboratory systems.

Even so, errors of replication do occur and these are termed 'mutations'. Mutations come in two broad categories: somatic cell mutations and germ line mutations. Somatic cells are those which make up the normal components of the body, and somatic cell mutations are therefore confined to the bulk of the tissues. Mutations of this sort are the cause of cancers, and from a forensic point of view are rarely, if ever, significant to an investigation. Germ line cells are those which pass on the genetic information from one generation to another, and mutations taking place here can substantially alter the picture in paternity cases. These mutations are a normal process and are, in fact, essential for evolution, both on a micro scale – such as population differences, and on a macro scale – which are differences between species.

Differences between populations can also be accounted for by a process called a 'founder' effect. This describes the situation where a small group breaks off from a larger population and, therefore, contains only a limited amount of the total possible range of genetic variation, resulting in an apparently distinct population.

As DNA analysis becomes a routine tool in paternity cases, it also becomes important to know something about the general rate of mutation events of the genetic systems being used. As we have seen, small changes in a gene may not result in any change in the gene product, so the mutation rates of blood groups, such as the ABO system, is infinitesimal, but the DNA which controls the blood groups will have a larger mutation rate. It is not entirely clear why, but some areas of the genome are mutational hot spots. This can be logically associated in some cases with the importance of a gene product: the greater the importance to the organism of the gene product the less likely it is that mutations will be tolerated. Areas of the genome used forensically tend to be in regions of the genome which are highly variable, being made up of non-coding areas, so that mutations are easily tolerated. So in terms of forensic measurement of variation, a great deal of the genome is of no use. Indeed, some areas of the genome are so highly conserved through evolutionary time that virtually the same gene sequence can be found in every animal and most plants, with only very minor changes.

4.2 Methods available for DNA analysis

There are many different ways in which information can be extracted from these variable areas of DNA. The method used is important because it has direct repercussions on the way in which results are expressed and, therefore, presented in court. It is important to understand the way in which these techniques are expressed because, although some countries stay at the forefront of technology, many countries use techniques which are no longer practised in the UK, but are still presented in courts elsewhere. These different methods of DNA analysis come into a number of broad categories, each of which will be described:

- variation in sequence length;
- variation in specific genes;
- variation in sequence repeat number; and
- variation in base sequence.

All of these require precise technology and conditions to produce an interpretable result, but whatever their precise requirements, they all result in some information which can aid personal identification. They all fall into the general description of DNA polymorphisms – that is, DNA that shows differences between individuals. Before any system can be implemented, it has to be based upon an established protocol and the details of all sequences, enzymes and probes published for public scrutiny. Publication must be in a peer-reviewed scientific journal. Other technical matters also have to be published, such as an adequate description to define the tested sequence and, if possible, the chromosomal location; proof of Mendelian inheritance, that is, proof that it is inherited from one generation to another in a predictable way; and some information regarding the frequencies at which the various forms are found. Besides these, a very important piece of information is the mutation rate. Mutations could result in apparent non-paternity by an individual passing on a germ line mutation, but should not significantly matter in material gathered from a scene of crime. This would include cases of rape where, although germ line cells (sperm) are tested, the mutation rate is so low that the mutation will be lost among all the non-mutated sperm. All this should also be reflected in the construction of a database which can be manipulated statistically to test for as many variables and possible problems as can be considered likely to occur.

Whichever of these techniques is used to produce a DNA profile result, the starting point has to be extracted DNA. There are many different ways in which this can be done, depending on the starting material. The easiest is carried out on epithelial cells. These are the sorts of cells which are found in mouth-wash samples or swabs from mucous membranes, such as vaginal or nasal cavities. They are relatively delicate and can be easily disrupted to yield their DNA into solution ready for processing. Other cell types are not so easily disrupted, and this is put to good use by the forensic scientists.

Sperm cells have a quite difficult task to perform in nature and consequently are protected and packaged so that they are able to actively seek out and fertilise the ovum. Sperm are therefore very robust cells, so if there is a mixture of cells, as would be expected in cases of rape where a vaginal swab will be taken producing both sperm and vaginal cells, the physical strength of DNA-carrying sperm heads can be capitalised upon. It will be apparent that if cells are present in a sample from two different individuals, then there will be a mixed DNA profile produced. It is sometimes possible to determine from a mixed profile the various components, but this will always remain a contentious issue, especially so when it may result in either a false acquittal or a false conviction.

The robustness of sperm cells can therefore be used as an added tool for the forensic scientist. The simplest example of this is to treat a sample from a rape case that is known, or thought to be, a mixture, such that the epithelial cells are destroyed, releasing their DNA into solution. It is then possible to remove the sperm cells by centrifugation, and subject them to a more rigorous DNA extraction, without the problems of having DNA from the victim making the results very difficult to interpret and producing a profile which may not truly reflect the DNA profile of the original sample.

Some of the later processing which takes place to produce a DNA profile is highly sensitive to the presence of proteins, and one of the most disruptive is haemoglobin, the oxygen-carrying material of red blood cells. For this reason it is of vital importance that by the time a profile is ready to be produced, the DNA is uncontaminated by other material from the cells.

4.2.1 Variation in DNA sequence length

Measurement of variation in sequence length is the earliest of the techniques of direct DNA analysis which became available to forensic science. The way in which this form of analysis takes place is simple in principle, but works on such a small scale that the theoretical basis of it has to be taken on trust.

This type of analysis is a multi-step procedure and is broadly described as restriction length polymorphism analysis, usually shortened to RFLP analysis. It is normally encountered in forensic applications described by the type of probe which is used to produce the result, so RFLP analysis will be described as single locus probe (SLP) or multilocus probe (MLP) analysis. Whether it is SLP or MLP, the starting material of the process is the same: extracted DNA.

Once DNA has been extracted it is treated enzymically using very specific enzymes, called restriction endonucleases. These cut DNA into different length sections by recognising very specific short sequences. These sequences are the important variables in producing both SLP and MLP profiles. In some individuals these recognition sequences may be missing, or there may be an additional one present; it only takes a single base change to do this because of the highly specific nature of the DNA cutting enzymes used.

Because the endonucleases will only cut a DNA strand at a very specific site, leaving the digestion process running for long periods will not alter the outcome, but if it is not run for long enough not all the DNA will have been cut and this can produce a false image. This digested solution then passes to the next stage of the process: electrophoresis.

Electrophoresis is the process whereby DNA fragments of different lengths can be separated. The medium in which this is done is a gel and depending upon the precise requirements of the analysis the material from which it is made up will be different. Whatever its composition the gel is a thin flat sheet, quite literally like a slab of jelly in both texture and appearance. By loading the DNA solution at one end and applying an electric current the DNA is driven through the gel, but the speed at which this migration takes place is dependent upon the length of the DNA fragments. Since small fragments travel faster than large ones, a gradual separation of the various pieces takes place. This process has to be timed so that all the DNA does not end up at one end of the gel in the same place. It is also important at this stage to have on the gel DNA fragments of known size, so that relatively accurate sizing of the fragments making up these profiles can take place.

The next phase of the process is to fix the DNA fragments so that they cannot move any more, the DNA being quite capable of passive diffusion through the gel in all directions once the current is turned off. This is carried out using a technique called 'Southern blotting'. In its simplest form, a piece of nylon membrane is laid over the top of the gel with absorbent paper towels on top of that. This draws the water in the gel, along with the DNA, up onto the nylon membrane where it can be immobilised by heating. The resultant membrane is an exact image of the gel, with all the DNA that was on the gel now on the membrane. As the DNA is now fixed in place it can be used and stored and reused as circumstances dictate. At this stage, it is still not possible to see the DNA on the gel, so we have to treat it to make it visible.

The DNA is now ready for probing, the process which will finally produce a visible DNA profile. Probes are short pieces of DNA which exactly complement a known sequence of DNA. They originally had a radioactive tag so that they could be easily detected, but chemical systems based on luminescence are more common now. By gently heating the membrane with the DNA bound to it in the presence of the probe and then cooling it, the probe binds reversibly to specific sections of the DNA. When the probed membrane is overlaid with a photographic plate, an image develops as a series of bands. With single locus probes there is either one band, if both chromosomes carrying the enzyme cutting site are the same, or if these are different and there are two versions, two different bands will be found. The reason for this is that single locus probes are so specific that they will only bind to a single site in the entire human genome. In comparison, multilocus probes are rather more promiscuous in their binding and will attach at a number of different complementary sites on the DNA scattered throughout the entire genome, resulting in a potentially very large number of bands in all individuals.

Because single locus probes are of relatively low discriminatory power, a panel of several probes is normally used, each one producing a low probability of a match, but collectively producing a relatively large probability when the data is added together. Each probe is used separately, and after each one the previous probe is stripped from the membrane by heating and washing and a new one applied. In contrast to this, one MLP will produce lots of bands simultaneously. It is these photographic images of the probed membrane which are used in court.

These methods of measuring a variation in sequence length have often been considered extremely effective as a means of either including or excluding a suspect from an investigation. They are good at this, but their real power lies in paternity cases where quite complicated family relationships can be worked out, because there is little or no possibility of subtle differences appearing in a closed group. This is not so in a wider population, where very small differences may result in non-exclusion. This is due to the measuring technique used to interpret these band patterns. This is crucial to both the interpretation and the acceptance of the results in court.

Interpreting either a panel of SLP data or an MLP profile is really a subjective activity. It has been standardised, but such standardisation that has been carried out is based on subjective agreement by the testing laboratories. It is simply not possible to be certain about the absolute sizes of these DNA fragments because the technology is both imprecise and inaccurate. This is not to say that such techniques are not valid, only that they are always worthy of question.

There are many technical issues which mitigate against the use of these probe systems in forensic cases. Multilocus probe systems were the first to be used in forensic cases and have provided a rich vein of argument. Most of these arguments stem from the technical issues surrounding them. It is not, for example, possible to be absolutely certain that two samples match, because the process of separating DNA fragments of this type is imprecise. This is for two main reasons. The first is simply that the migration of large pieces of DNA in an electric field is very difficult to control accurately, and in fact no two runs will be exactly the same. This can be due to any of several reasons, such as the small variation of transmitting current, differences in the conductivity of the gel, and the rigidity of the gel. Control of these is always attempted, but not all variation can be excluded. The second, and more important, reason is that these pieces of DNA may vary in size from a few hundred base pairs to more than 10,000 base pairs, and a match is declared if two bands fall into a specified window. This can be defined in many ways, such as a window ranging in size by +/–2.5% – if it is within that range it is an inclusion, and out of that range it is an exclusion, or mismatch. The figure of 2.5% reflects the range of measurements which can be found on a single sample which is repeatedly analysed. But this does not take into account that there is always a possibility that changes may take place within any given variable region which is smaller than this, so an apparent inclusion could in fact be an exclusion; there is no way in which this can be demonstrated because the technology employed has an accuracy which is less than the possible variation. This problem has been addressed in later techniques, but a brief look at some judicial comments on the subject of this manner of DNA analysis will serve to emphasise the point that even under the most rigorous conditions, singe locus and multilocus probe systems are really not suitable for forensic applications; there are simply too many variables which cannot be controlled in a routine laboratory.

It has been suggested that there was unseemly haste in the introduction of early DNA profiling techniques, a view which is now quite widely held, based on the mistakes which occurred in the early court cases using DNA. Later systems, which had a far better theoretical basis, and with it a far better understanding of the biology and genetics, tend not to have the same shortcomings, but the results still need close scrutiny.

A good example of the way in which an inappropriate rush to implementation of this technology has caused problems can be found in some of the early cases in which it was used. These originally stemmed from the US, and three examples serve to demonstrate the pitfalls of not having adequate safeguards and quality auditing systems of laboratories available, whether private or public. This includes the essential ability of the defence, when faced with DNA evidence, being able to appoint their own expert, either to audit the results or to organise their own independent testing of the samples.

In New York in 1987, Hamilton Neysmith was charged with rape on the basis of an identification made by the victim, a notoriously unreliable method of personal identification. At his instigation, a blood sample was tested from him for comparison with semen samples originating from the rapist, and the testing laboratory was Lifecodes. The initial result was stated as a mismatch – that is, Neysmith could not be the originator of the crime sample. This excluded him from the crime. If this had been taken as an absolute result, then justice would not have been served. An astute observer from the prosecutors' office stated quite correctly that he may not have sent his own blood, so a second sample was ordered to be taken by the judge in the case. At this point, Lifecodes stated that the two blood samples came from two different people. A demand by Neysmith resulted in a third sample being tested by a different laboratory, which confirmed the original result that there was an exclusion, but also an admission by Lifecodes that they had made and error. This had a considerable knock on effect. In 1988 in a case, *New York v McNamara* (1989) 339 Nature 501–05, a request for a DNA test to be carried out was denied because the testing agency had been inaccurate and therefore unreliable. Even so, DNA profiling was used in the same district quite soon afterwards. In *New York v Castro* (1989) 545 NY Supp 985 (SC, NY) the same testing agency, Lifecodes, produced a DNA profile which declared a match between a blood spot on a watch and the victim. Castro later admitted that he was guilty of the murder, but in the interim the DNA profile results were picked apart, and having seen the autoradiographs used in the case I am not surprised.

This resulted in an enormous debate which culminated in calls for the extremes of either abandoning DNA evidence, or embracing DNA evidence without question. In the UK in the case of *R v Hammond* (1992) unreported, 7 December, at the Central Criminal Court, the judge ruled that the DNA evidence was inadmissible. This was followed up two years later in 1994, in the Court of Appeal (Criminal Division), in the case of *R v Gordon* [1995] Crim LR 413. The appeal was upheld on the basis that there was uncertainty as to the quality of the Home Office analysis. In this particular case no doubt was expressed as to the validity of DNA evidence as a whole; it was just suggested that the variation could not be determined on the membrane and that the database which was used to determine the probability of finding the same single locus profile in the general Afro-Caribbean population was not soundly based. This was of considerable significance, because it galvanised the Home Office into creating a considerably larger database for each recognisably different racial group. It also investigated possibilities of defining racial group from the profile. What became apparent quite quickly was that for most bands, the frequencies did not vary a great deal between racial types, but the accumulated frequencies could be quite different.

These databases, one for each system used, were the subject of the same criticism as were the examples taken into court. It had to be one for each system used because the results are dependent upon two fundamentals: the enzyme used to cut the DNA into sections, and the probe which is then used to bind to specific sequences. If either one of these two is different, the end result will also be different. These primarily revolved around the difficulty of being certain that the bands which were said to be represented covered the whole range of possible sizes, and how easy they were to compare, but also the possibility of the presence of anomalous bands was addressed. Anomalous bands are ones which cannot be explained and therefore make the entire analysis difficult to explain, or even to justify as having worked properly.

Dealing with anomalous bands first, a report of the National Research Council in the US made some very important points regarding this problem in SLP profiles. What they broadly said is that SLP profiles can show additional bands for a number of reasons. It should be remembered that SLP profiles of an individual should only ever show a maximum of two bands, unlike MLP profiles, which are profligate in their bands. SLP profiles should, therefore, always be fully recorded, and any anomalies described completely. These may be due to contamination of a sample, either at the crime scene or laboratory, or due to failures in what is a technically demanding procedure being carried out in a laboratory where processing such samples is regarded as routine. This same report suggested that the window of resolution should be only +/–2%, rather than the previously described 2.5%. Even so, this leaves a large true variation possible without it being necessary to comment upon it. These, and many other reasons, resulted in a continuing search for a reliable alternative to techniques which were highly subjective in interpretation. One such was the 'dot blot', a presence or absence system similar in result to blood tests, but more sensitive. This will be discussed in the next section.

4.2.2 Variation in a specific gene: presence or absence assays

When it was felt that the first techniques of DNA analysis were too contentious to pursue further, other methods were looked for. One of the first methods involved an entirely new procedure to manipulate DNA which has resulted in unprecedented sensitivity of analysis.

This new method of manipulating DNA is called the polymerase chain reaction (PCR). The process was described in 1985 by Kary Mullis, a somewhat idiosyncratic scientist, at the meeting of the American Society of Human Genetics. So important was this to genetics and molecular biology that he was awarded the Nobel Prize in 1993 for this work.

PCR works by mimicking the way in which cells themselves replicate DNA. The implications of this are profound. Most enzymes are easily destroyed by heat, but there are some which come from organisms living around very hot deep sea vents which are stable. One of these is called DNA polymerase, and can be induced to replicate DNA in a test tube. The process is essentially a simple repetitive cycling of changing conditions. There are limits to the length of DNA which can be successfully replicated without errors, so for forensic applications short sequences are normally used. In the test tube the essential ingredients for replication of DNA using PCR are:

- Target DNA – this is a solution of all the DNA that has been extracted from all the cells in the sample. The extracted DNA will contain a great deal of material which will not be used; it is the target DNA which is of importance. However, we do not need to know the exact base sequence of the target DNA which is to be measured, but we do need to know the exact base sequence of the DNA which is at either side of the target. This is because we can determine the length of a strand quite easily, as long as we know from where we are counting and this requires knowledge of the start and stop points. It is analogous to counting stitches in knitting. If you know that the group of plain stitches you are interested in come between a set of pearl stitches, you have the exact start and stop points for counting. The base sequence which we need to know may only be 20 or 30 bases long.
- DNA primers – these have to be complementary sequences to the known sequence flanking the target DNA.
- DNA polymerase enzyme.
- A mixture of individual DNA bases which can be incorporated in the right order to create a new DNA strand using the old one as a template.

When all these are mixed together, replication can proceed. This is started by heating the solution up to approximately 90°C. This causes the two strands of the target DNA double helix to melt, or come apart. When the solution is then cooled to about 50°C the primers anneal, or join, to their complementary sequence. At this point we have a section of single stranded DNA with a primer attached, making a short piece of double stranded DNA. When this is heated to 70°C, the polymerase enzyme starts with the primer and proceeds along the single stranded DNA, using it as a template to replicate an entire new double strand. So where there had been one double strand of target DNA we now have two, each of which is made up of one half of the original and a completely artificial complementary strand.

By repeating this cycle the old and new strands separate at 90°C, another primer attaches itself, and replication at 70°C results in four strands, so that at every round the number of strands of DNA is doubled. So starting with a single target we get 2, 4, 8, 16, 32, 64, 128, 256, 512, 1024, 2048, 4096. So after 20 cycles, from a single original there could be just over 1,000,000 copies which could be analysed further. Very quickly the large pieces of original target DNA are completely swamped in a sea of artificially replicated target DNA which are all short and of known size. It can be readily appreciated that with this exponential increase in target DNA it is possible to start with very small samples and produce a reliable and consistent result.

One way in which this technique can be applied is in production of dot blots. This is a technique which can be used when the PCR is known to produce a finite range of different products which do not differ in length, but do differ significantly in the internal sequence of the target DNA. Under such circumstances, it is necessary to know the sequence variable region so that a probe can be constructed. An example of this is the DQa system. This is a system that makes use of a variable region in a gene on a chromosome which codes for proteins which help recognise invading organisms, such as bacteria. It is known to contain several different alleles, or varieties of DNA, of which four are easily tested. Four spots of the PCR products are immobilised onto a nylon membrane and then denatured by heat. At this point each one of the PCR spots has a different probe added, one for each possible type. The probes in this case have a reporter molecule attached, so when cooled down and rinsed only the probe binding to its exact counterpart in the PCR products will remain. The reporter molecule is then developed to give a coloured product. Essentially this removes the subjectivity of interpretation, because the dots either develop a colour or they do not. However, they are dependent on knowing the exact sequence so that a probe can be produced, but perhaps their greatest limitation is that they have a very limited range of alleles, or different types of DNA, which can be measured. In the case of DQa, any person could have a maximum of two coloured dots if the two chromosomes carried different forms, and a minimum of one if they were the same, so starting with four different types the maximum number of possible combinations is 10, and although some are commoner than others, this is not very discriminatory from a forensic point of view. Even with the introduction of two subtypes, bringing the total allele number to six, the number of possible outcomes is still only 21.

What is wanted is something with the same objectivity, the same or better sensitivity, but far greater discriminatory power. This goal has yielded some very powerful methods, but most of them either require so much material that they are impractical or so much skill that routine laboratory use would be virtually impossible. The common systems currently in use combine very nearly all of these requirements.

4.2.3 Variation in repeats of a DNA base sequence: short tandem repeats (STRs)

One of the ways in which it was possible to get around the inherently contentious nature of DNA analysis, which relied too much on personal opinion, was to automate the system. As we shall see, this has not entirely worked, but has improved the situation considerably. The other aspect to be addressed is low discriminatory power; there is little point in having a completely reliable and unquestionable system if it does not tell you anything about the origin of the sample.

Short tandem repeat (STR) analysis addressed these points, but also allowed for a greater level of development as our understanding increased. Part of the importance of STR analysis in forensic science stems from the very simple premise upon which it is based and the very simple method of analysis used to give a result. The premise upon which it is based is that scattered throughout the genome of most organisms are areas of DNA which do not code for anything, although that is not to say that they are not of importance in gene control and evolution. It should also be remembered that this apparently simple observation was in fact hard-won over many years by pooling much research. These sections of DNA often contain short sequences which are repeated. These can be two, three or more bases long, but the important point is that they vary in number between individuals, so the simple method of analysis is to count the number of repeats and just say which section of DNA the result came from.

The practical issues of doing this are a little more complicated, but an appreciation of them will give a better understanding of the results as they are presented in court. The first question must be what are STRs? Embedded within genes are regions that are made up of nothing more than repeat motifs. Since DNA is constructed entirely from four bases, designated A, T, C, G, the repeats can be of any type, but some are not helpful. For example, it was quickly realised that repeats of only two bases caused problems in accurate counting of them because of errors introduced by the PCR process itself and, of course, this would be exacerbated further if it was simply a repeat of a single base. Another reason that it may not be helpful to use some of these repeat sequences in forensic applications is that they are inherently unstable. Indeed they are so unstable and so genetically problematic that some of them are the cause of several very unpleasant inherited diseases, such as Huntingdon's chorea, which is a late-onset degenerative disease causing premature death. It is inherited as a dominant trait. Fragile X syndrome, resulting in severe learning disability, has a rather strange mode of inheritance which caused a great deal of confusion to geneticists involved in research on this condition but also involves repeat sequences.

Short tandem repeats are repeats of between three and six bases; if there are more than six bases in a repeat they tend not to be called STRs, although the boundary is not absolute between STRs and ordinary repeat sequences. Given the four bases available, an STR would be made up of any combination, repeated any number of times. So examples might be ACG ACG ACG ACG or GTAA GTAA GTAA GTAA GTAA. But what would not work would be AAAAAAAAAA or CACACACACACA. The multiple repeat of A or any other single base would be extremely difficult to replicate accurately, as would the two base repeat sequence. But the bigger problem would be that determining the number of repeats, even with the very best equipment, would be highly contentious. The reason for this is quite straightforward: counting only ten bases would require an error rate of 10% to generate an incorrect number; with 100 bases an error rate of 1% would introduce an inaccuracy; when it came to 1,000 an error rate of 0.1% would result in a questionable result. The traditional way of getting around these problems is to repeat the process several times and take the modal figure. This is simply the number which turns up most frequently. The reason for using this rather than taking the mean value of adding all the results together and dividing by the number of tests is that this would result in a nonsense value of a fraction: say, purely for example, 92.4, and it is obviously absurd to pretend to have a fraction of a base. Even taking a modal value into court would generate considerable argument and would render comparison between laboratories extremely difficult.

Most of the STR systems currently in forensic use are based upon a repeat of four bases, each STR generating a single number. Consulting a frequency database for that particular STR gives a frequency for that number of repeats appearing in that STR in the population. By combining several of these STR results, a progressively decreasing value for the probability of finding this combination of values is found. The statistical aspects of STR analysis and database comparison will be dealt with in more detail in Chapter 5.

When originally introduced, STR analysis only used four different STRs. These set the trend in naming, that is, the STR taking the name of the gene in which the STR is found; unfortunately it has not proved possible to continue this because many STRs are found in anonymous regions of the genome that do not seem to belong to specific genes. There was also an early trend to prefix the name with HUM, standing for human, but since these STRs do not appear to occur any where else other than in humans this has been dropped. These four original STRs were a rather mixed lot, some being particularly uninformative, so it was not uncommon to find probability figures for finding the same profile in the population by chance of one in 250. Since the previous systems managed probabilities of several million, these early attempts at using STR analysis were rigorously questioned in terms of exactly what this figure can be interpreted as meaning. Currently there are 10 STRs routinely used to produce a DNA profile, which can generate very large probabilities indeed. The figures now produced rival those of the earlier systems in running into tens or even hundreds of millions. The problems with these sorts of figures, as we shall see later, is one of perception of meaning.

Perhaps the greatest problems with STR analysis come from the possibility of animal contamination giving a result, and bad practice contaminating a sample with someone else's DNA. The first problem has been tackled by simply testing the systems against as many species as are likely to be found associated with a crime scene. These broadly fall into two categories: food species and commensal species. Food species are obvious and are the most obvious potential origin of contamination in a household. Meat – sheep, pig, cow and poultry – are the main ones, and can be tested against the STR systems being used to see if they produce a result. As far as we know, vegetable products do not produce a result because of the genes involved, but the comments regarding meat and other potential animal material also holds true for plant material. Although in general the possibility of a problem with food material is not likely to be of great importance, there is always the possibility that something has been overlooked in this regard. It is true that common foodstuffs have been clearly excluded as producing a result from currently used systems, but if an individual has an unusual diet, and it must be remembered that some individuals and some groups do, the question should always be asked as to whether these strange food products have been screened to rule them out of the picture.

A greater potential problem is from commensal species. These constitute all those species which live with us and from which we are supposed to materially neither gain nor lose. This definition was created in contrast to parasites, from which the host loses, or symbiosis, where both parties gain. So although it could be argued that household pets are either parasites or symbionts, depending upon your outlook, generally this group of organisms can be viewed as commensal, as can most of the infesting organisms that share our living space. So testing should be carried out on household pets of all types, again some of which can seem rather odd, my own choice of pets being snakes, for example. But it is also important to test the less desirable sharers of our space such as cockroaches, rats and mice. In some cases these species will represent a considerable component of the background DNA present in a household. All of these things are time consuming and costly to guard against, but at the same time essential to demonstrate the robustness of the system being used.

Although this is currently the system of choice in forensic applications, STR profiling will be superseded. It does at the moment seem to be in an unassailable position as it is the basis of so many forensic databases, but it should be remembered that it is based on counting the numbers of repeats which are present in a given stretch of DNA; how much better to know the DNA sequence complete. This is a far away goal and one which would never work for most forensic applications because the DNA available is usually degraded, but variations in DNA sequence is being used to some extent.

4.2.4 Variation in base sequence and direct analysis of DNA sequence

We can easily think that knowing the complete DNA sequence of an individual tells us everything about that individual, but this a false premise. Biology has many more surprises up its sleeve than simple reductionism would allow us to believe. So even if we were able to sequence an entire genome, that is, all the DNA of an individual, we would still not know that person, but small changes in DNA sequence can be tracked and noted for forensic uses.

The simplest method of looking at changes in base sequence would be to target a single base out of the entire genome of 3,000,000,000 bases and see how it varies between individuals. This apparently outrageous possibility is in fact relatively easy to carry out. The process is called single nucleotide polymorphism analysis, reduced to SNP analysis, but often in conversation called snip analysis. This is most likely to take over from STR analysis in the construction of DNA databases.

The basis of SNP analysis is that throughout the genome, in active genes and non-active areas, there are single bases changes. These occur at the rate of approximately one every 1,000 bases. If they happen to be in an active gene then they can be responsible for disease, but if they are in a non-active area they tend to be benign.

To measure the presence of an SNP it is necessary to know both the nature of the expected change and the sequence of DNA on either side of the SNP. By modifying the process of the PCR it is possible to terminate the growing DNA chain when it comes to a point of mutation – the SNP. When these PCR products are run out on a gel there are two possibilities. If the person whose sample is being tested is homozygous, that is, both chromosomes carry the same base at exactly the same point on their DNA, there will be a single band. But, if the person is heterozygous, that is, the two chromosomes have different bases at exactly the same point, then there will be two bands.

As can be appreciated, a single SNP analysis is, in a forensic context, really rather uninformative. However, vast numbers of these can be combined to generate very large probabilities with very great ease. There are some ethical questions which have to be addressed with SNP analysis, because it would appear inevitable that unless very great care is taken forensic analysis will also result in inadvertent analysis of disease susceptibility for some genetic conditions. Of course, SNP analysis is really a shorthand version of the ultimate method of detecting DNA variation, which is sequencing the whole genome.

DNA sequencing can now be carried out far faster and cheaper than ever before; when it was first attempted the results were slow to produce and it was a highly skilful process. It was also true that the results were not always easy to interpret. The technology behind the process was complicated and long winded. With the advent of automation, fuelled by the race to sequence the entire genome, commercial interest brought large teams to the development of equipment and specialist reagents which cut the time to sequence the genome to a fraction of what it would have been. Even so, the possibility of sequencing an entire genome from a small scene of crime sample remains, at the moment, only a distant possibility. If it were possible to do this there would also be the question of acceptable error rates, since it is inconceivable that 3,000,000,000 bases could be sequenced reliably and repeatably. The question also remains as to why it would be necessary, as we know that large sections of the genome do not vary, and since we are looking for variation between individuals, that makes them rather uninformative. Part of the drive towards sequencing is fuelled by the belief that it would be possible to determine physical features from the genome. This thought belies the complexity of the interactions between different genes. This interaction is called 'multifactorial inheritance', a term which reflects that there may be more, many more, than one gene involved in determining some characters. Indeed it is not only genetics which influence an outcome of appearance, although the genetic component can be driven by several different genes. The environmental influence can be seen at a low level in identical twins, where it is impossible for genetics to predict the fingerprints. This is manifestly so since identical twins, with identical DNA, do not have identical fingerprints. At a rather larger scale it would only confuse matters if it was said that a DNA result predicted a long straight nose, but the individual had, for whatever reason, broken his nose and changed its shape. This is not as silly as it may seem: many people tint or dye their hair, wear wigs, have their teeth straightened or change their shape by diet or exercise, as perfectly acceptable social behaviour. Generally speaking, it would not be a very useful activity at this stage to look into these aspects. They represent a molecular answer to a question of genetics which is far more complicated than is generally understood. It is similar to being given a complete list of car parts and being expected to tell what make it is.

There is a forensic use of sequence data which is already of very great power when used in the right context: this is a method of sequencing a very short section of mitochondrial DNA (mtDNA).

Mitochondrial DNA is found in every cell and is located exclusively within mitochondria. This is the energy powerhouse of the cell and is quite independent of the cell nucleus. It does quite literally generate the energy which keeps you going from the sugars which you eat. Mitochondria also have a generally agreed origin which sounds bizarre but is probably true: in the mists of time one form of bacteria invaded another, each being able to complement the other metabolically. The result of this symbiosis is that we all have mitochondria, indeed we could not live without them, and mitochondria have their own DNA. Mitochondrial DNA takes the form of a distorted circle of double stranded DNA which is approximately 16,570 bases long.

There is a recognised wisdom that mitochondrial DNA (mtDNA) is only inherited from the mother. This is not strictly true, but the thinking behind the idea is interesting. The ovum is a relatively large cell and contains a large number of mitochondria. By comparison, sperm is little more than an encapsulated nucleus with a single large mitochondrion providing energy for the flagella, which is the tail which propels the sperm along. It is not unusual for the mitochondrion to enter the ovum at the same time as the nucleus of the sperm. This should not usually cause any problems with the analysis of mtDNA because the maternal mitochondria seem to be preferentially replicated within the cell.

The maternal inheritance of mtDNA means that it is not easily possible to use mtDNA in criminal cases since all children, of both sexes, will have the same mtDNA as their mother and, what is more, all the descendants originating from the female line will have the same mtDNA. This will carry on potentially for ever, but in practice there will be a slow process of change as mutations occur occasionally from one generation to the next; there is generally no paternal input to mtDNA.

As can be appreciated from this, using mtDNA analysis in a criminal case could be a source of confusion in the courts. But worse, it could implicate a completely innocent sibling as the culprit because mtDNA comparison between a scene of crime sample and any of the siblings of the source of the sample will produce a perfect match. However, it is possible to use mtDNA to unravel family relationships when all other methods have failed, but only in very special circumstances. For example, it would not help in paternity cases, and usually there is not a problem with disputed maternity. But what of the cases where remains of a person are found that are very badly decayed? In such a situation nuclear DNA, the material usually looked at first, is quite likely to be unusable because it has been badly damaged by microbes of all sorts. This is likely to happen because nuclear DNA is associated with the soft parts of the body – tissues and organs which break down quickly. It is true that nuclear DNA can be found in bone marrow of long bones, but these too can be susceptible to damage because of the open nature of bone marrow.

On the other hand, although mtDNA is also found in all metabolically active cells, it is also found in hair shafts and bone itself, rather than the interior bone marrow. These two materials, hair and bone, survive very well for extremely long periods of time in very adverse conditions, and under some circumstances, such as mummification, for thousands of years. It is certain that in cases of exhumation of human remains mtDNA can be extremely useful.

Probably one of the most spectacular successes of mtDNA analysis involves the resolution of the question of the survival of Anastasia, daughter of Czar Nicholas II of Russia, and the identification of the Romanov family, the royal lineage of Russia. The story started with the disappearance of the Russian royal family during the revolution of 1918. According to well documented local records, the Romanovs had been killed by firing squad on 16 July 1918 at Ekaterinberg; the bodies had been dumped in a mineshaft and then two days later buried in a shallow grave.

Decades later this grave was discovered. After 70 years in the ground the nuclear DNA was badly damaged, but could be partially analysed using STRs. Mitochondrial analysis confirmed the presence of the Tsar and Tsarina, three of their children and four other unknown adults. The daughters were Marie, Tatiana and Olga, so two members of the family were absent – Alexei and Grand Duchess Anastasia. Since Alexei was a haemophiliac and nobody claimed to be him, it was assumed that he too had perished.

But the lack of Anastasia's body fuelled a debate regarding the existence of a person claiming to be Anastasia. If such a claim could be substantiated the political and financial implications would be enormous. A woman known as Anna Anderson claimed to be Anastasia in 1921, when she was in a Berlin mental hospital, and even when she died in the US in 1984 there was no reliable method of DNA analysis which could be used. Luck played a part in the process, as Anna Anderson had been taken into hospital in 1979 and had had a small bowel biopsy taken which had been stored for many years. By using STR analysis it was possible to compare remnant DNA from the Romanov bones and show that Anna Anderson was not a member of the family.

Scientists went on to show that mitochondrial sequences from Anna Anderson also ruled her out conclusively. In this particular case it was carried out by comparing her mtDNA with that of the Duke of Edinburgh, a known maternal descendent of the Tsarina. Had they been related, the Duke of Edinburgh and Anna Anderson would have had the same mtDNA.

Mitochondrial DNA analysis was then used to unravel exactly who she really was. It had been suggested that her real identity was that of Franzisca Schanzkowska, a Pole. A documented great-nephew on the maternal side of

Franzisca Schanzkowska was known and his mtDNA analysis matched exactly that of Anna Anderson.

As can be appreciated, mtDNA has many uses, but they tend to be associated with ancient remains where normal methods of nuclear DNA analysis fails to provide adequate data for a complete picture to emerge. Under such circumstances, mtDNA analysis can help to clarify the position. There are some situations when mtDNA analysis will give no information at all, even though it is the only analysable material available. One such situation is in cases of disputed paternity requiring an exhumation. I have been involved in such a case where a discretely wealthy man died and was buried. Some time later, after probate, it was discovered that the estate was far greater than was ever imagined. At this point a child was produced on behalf of which claims were made against the estate. Depending upon the state of the ground and time of year of burial, nuclear DNA may remain available for partial or complete analysis, but even if the exhumed was the father of the child they would have different mtDNA. So although it survives longer than nuclear DNA, being found in bones and hair shafts, it would be completely uninformative.

SUMMARY

As techniques of DNA analysis have progressed from the indirect methods of blood grouping to systems which require knowledge of exact sequences, the discriminatory power for the forensic scientist has waxed and waned. What is certain is that overall the change in techniques has, and will, increase the ability of the forensic science community to discriminate between individuals.

Early uses of DNA analysis were based upon variations in sequence length using enzymes and probes. This complicated procedure required highly trained technical staff and was both time consuming, meaning that results could take weeks to prepare, and consequently expensive. These assays were also subjective in their method of analysis, so arguments over interpretation of results took up a considerable amount of court time. Presence or absence assays were of low discriminatory power on their own, so a more reliable system was searched for. This was short tandem repeat (STR) analysis. This is currently the method of choice used by all major forensic science services in the world. It has become extensively automated and produces results which are so repeatable that results can be passed between testing laboratories both within and between countries for comparison.

There are undoubtedly better systems on the horizon, but they will always have their own drawbacks. Not least of which are the ethical questions which will arise from simply being able to demand a sample from any arrested individual and then being able to carry out any test which the operator sees fit, even to the diagnosis of a life threatening disease.

Another aspect of DNA analysis which has developed is mitochondrial DNA (mtDNA) analysis. This is inherited through the maternal line, so all siblings share the same mtDNA with their mother, their father having a different mtDNA sequence. This can be extremely useful in some very specific circumstances. These would include following a matrilineal line, or in cases where there may have been multiple fathers for a group of children all claiming the same father. Mitochondrial DNA analysis is also useful in exhumations because the long bones, teeth and hair shafts all contain mitochondria and are particularly resistant to decay. Such methods of analysis tend to be associated with ancient remains, but have been used in legal cases, both criminal and civil on several occasions.

CHAPTER 5

PATERNITY TESTS AND CRIMINAL CASES

INTRODUCTION

The two major areas in which DNA analysis is involved in court proceedings are criminal cases and paternity disputes. Although the mechanics of DNA analysis does not alter between these two, the way in which the resultant data is used does vary quite considerably. These differences start with the initial question which is being asked. It is important that the right question is asked for the right case. There is, for example, little point in asking the same question in a paternity case as in a criminal case. A question asked in a criminal case might be 'did the sample originate from this individual?' which in a paternity dispute would be meaningless, since we already know where the sample came from. It is unfortunate that very often results are presented in court without the exact question which needs to be asked being explicitly stated. This is the central element of this chapter: the right questions for the particular case with which you are faced.

Although not the sole province of DNA evidence, the questions asked are relevant to all forms of scientific evidence and its interpretation. There are very many ways in which information from test results can be presented in court, but it is beholden of the experts to maintain a standard of presentation upon which other experts can agree, and of course, to ensure that the court has results which they can both trust and understand. This constraint has led to some simplified methods of data presentation, leaving out some of the details of the analysis. This is not to denigrate the intelligence or perception of the court, advocates, judges or jury, but it is a reflection of the unnecessary complexity that can be generated by scientific evidence unless great care is taken by the experts involved to explain without recourse to jargon. This attempt at complete explanation was tried in the first cases where DNA evidence was used, but the result was an over-long explanation of bewildering complexity which did little to clarify the situation for the court.

In this chapter we will look at the way in which scientific evidence can be viewed and interpreted in court. It will also deal with the value of scientific evidence, sometimes overstated, and the way in which the probative value of expert evidence can be assessed, both formally and informally. It will therefore inevitably deal with the much maligned area of statistics. It should be remembered that statistics is not a matter of numeracy, but of trying to put as much of an objective value on a result as is possible.

5.1 How relevant is scientific evidence?

Genetics is an unusual subject as a source of expert evidence, because unlike, say, fire investigators, it should not be a matter of opinion. This, unfortunately, is not always the case. It has been known for arguments to arise between experts because of trivial differences in results being interpreted as fundamental differences. When there really is a fundamental difference between experts, it is usually possible to resolve the questions by conference.

To look at DNA specifically, this sort of evidence could on the face of it be regarded as 'ideal' evidence in so far as it is thought to discriminate absolutely between individuals. Unfortunately there will always be a residual doubt about this discriminatory power, as we have discussed; it can never be ruled out that two unrelated individuals share the same DNA profile and possibly even the very same DNA sequence. If this situation arose it would add to the urban myth of the doppel-ganger – a true double – a situation so unlikely as to be implausible. This is quite different to identical twins where DNA is shared in common, as they can be thought of as clones of each other. A genetic double would effectively be an unrelated identical twin: not only an oxymoron but an absurd idea.

Much has been written about the assessment of evidence, but it is worth reviewing this with a specific slant on DNA evidence. While all evidence which is relevant to a case will alter the opinion of the jury, some will undoubtedly be held as more significant than others, and DNA is just such evidence. It is often the perception, an incorrect perception, by the public that DNA evidence is infallible. There are several reasons for this being true. Besides obvious questions of reliability in the transmission of samples from crime scenes and tested individuals to the testing laboratory, and practice in the laboratory itself, there is also the major question of statistical reliability. Even if someone states, based upon recognised calculation, that the probability of this sample having *not* come from a specified individual is one in 10,000,000, this does not rule out the possibility that the sample did originate from another person.

At this point we have to introduce some statistical concepts. It should not be assumed that statistics is all mathematical, as with a little effort it is possible to see through the mathematical statements to the very core, and therefore the true meaning of the numerical results which are presented to the advocate.

There are broadly two ways of expressing the likelihood of an event. These are *probability* and *odds*. They originate from the same data, but each method of expression has good points, and places where they are best used. Odds, for example, are routinely used in stating the perceived probability of a particular horse winning a race. In this case the odds can be extremely misleading because they are calculated before the outcome is known, whereas in forensic cases the outcome is known and we want to know the likelihood of an event having taken place in a specific way. Put another way, we can say that odds on a horse race is betting on the outcome, but in a criminal or paternity dispute we know the outcome so we are betting on the events which led up to it. This is an extremely difficult position to be in, as there may be any number of possible scenarios which could end in the result we already know, but only one of them is correct. Unfortunately, only those present at the time will know the truth and even here errors may be made. Identification evidence by a victim of rape, for example, is known to be questionable, and disguise is not unknown. Even more extreme is that of a murder victim with a single assailant, where there may be no possible way that the truth comes out, unless the aggressor describes exactly what happened. So we have to use a system of probabilities, or statistical calculations, to try and work out the most likely events which took place.

Now consider, a proportion of jurors will have a clear grasp of odds, but not necessarily the concomitant probability. So it may well be of value to state the odds, rather than a probability, that an event took place in the manner stated. The problem with this is that 'odds' are seen in two ways which are detrimental to their use in court. The first is, admittedly only from my own research, that odds are seen as imprecise. This may be associated with the second perceived problem of stating odds: they are seen as predictive, that is, operating in the future. The reason for this is that they are inextricably linked to horse and dog racing where odds are calculated for an event, that is, the likelihood of a specific horse winning a race. But odds are just as good as probability and are often more easily understood because of the exposure of individuals to odds rather than probabilities in daily life, if only from betting.

The way in which odds are calculated in forensic applications is very simple and uses probabilities as the first point of contact. First, though, a clarifying word on probabilities. Probability has a very straightforward expression, ranging from 0 to 1.0 is a statement of certainty that something did not, or would not, happen, and a probability of 1 is a statement of certainty of an event taking place, or having taken place while a probability of 0 is certainty that it did not. Using this logic it is quickly seen that if an event, perhaps a rape or murder, has taken place, the probability of that event is, *de facto*, 1. These are posterior odds; what is wanted in forensic applications is a statement of probability, or odds, that a particular individual took part in the event, not that it happened in the first place.

One of the problems of both odds and probability is the perception of uncertainty associated with them. Odds are seen as a means of guessing an outcome, whereas probability is seen as a means of determining the outcome. Although these statements are different they are both wrong. In forensic applications both odds and probability are means of determining the same thing: the likelihood that a hypothesis is true.

To convert from probability to odds is easy. Simply take the probability – a figure which, remember, must be between 0 and 1 – and then using this number, take it from 1 and drop the fraction. There you have odds from probability. An example:

PROBABILITY	0.4
1 – PROBABILITY	0.6
ODDS ARE THEREFORE	6 to 4 in favour of the statement.

To work backwards from odds to probability is the reverse process, and although it can be an interesting exercise it does not necessarily add to the information available to the court – just to the level of confusion felt by a jury.

It should be incumbent on the advocate to make sure that whatever the court needs to know it is put in a way that the jury can understand easily.

In the case of odds which are sometimes described as 'evens' this is represented as a probability of 0.5, or sometimes as 50/50. Such a probability can tells us nothing about an assertion because it is exactly the same probability of it being true as false. It is often thought that statistical analysis is based upon multiple events, and in many cases it is, such as the probability of pulling an ace from a pack of cards is 4/52, the probability of pulling another ace from the same pack is now 3/51. But in forensic applications it is single events which are important, so the questions which are asked are quite different: not the probability of an event taking place, but the probability of an explanation of an event which has already taken place – effectively the probability that a set of circumstances which are used to explain an event are the most likely. So probabilities used in court are an attempt to objectively quantify which of any number of different scenarios took place at a crime scene where, in a murder for example, only the victim and assailant know the truth: the victim has no voice and the assailant is going to try and obfuscate the situation. So to make odds and probabilities relevant to the scientific evidence and help the court understand what took place, we need to be clear what statistics can and cannot tell us.

5.2 Old statistics and new statistics

Into this situation we have introduced a form of statistics which can help to clarify the position, but to start with it is worth considering why statistics can confuse rather than help. As stated previously, probability is the cornerstone of statistics, but very often the way in which probabilities are expressed is simply mind boggling and relies on repeated experiments.

The mathematics of statistical analysis is often very straightforward, but unfortunately it answers questions that we are simply not interested in. For example, according to Karl Popper, any scientific hypothesis has to be falsifiable, that is, disprovable. This is actually an axiomatic statement of science, although scientists do not always realise that this is what they are doing. Basically, a hypothesis has to be set up which can be disproved, rather than proved. This is called the 'null hypothesis' and this is what is tested.

There is little point in saying 'there are fairies at the bottom of my garden' because however much I search for them, if I do not find them it can always be said that I have not looked hard enough. Put another way, this hypothesis is impossible to disprove, but can be proven. If we take the alternative hypothesis that there are no fairies at the bottom of my garden, this can be disproved and alternatively the hypothesis accepted as a valid statement. So, in more complicated situations where the outcome is not simply yes or no, in drug trials for example, where the outcome depends on the individuals involved, a statistical analysis has to be undertaken. This often starts with a null hypothesis which broadly states that the drug will not change the course of the condition. Now, because of the nature of very large drug trials it is possible that some individuals will recover with abnormal speed without medical intervention of any sort. Consequently, a statistical level at which the null hypothesis is rejected has to be set up, and this is called the 'confidence interval'. If a confidence interval of 95% is quoted, all that this tells us is that with lots of repeated trials the unknown result, perhaps the speed of recovery, would lie within the confidence limit 95% of the time. As can be easily appreciated, this is not very helpful in forensic applications where each event requiring DNA analysis is essentially unique. When it comes to databases, which will be discussed later, this is not quite true.

Difficulty regarding interpretation of statistical results is surprisingly common and, quite frankly, unnecessary. The techniques of analysis used for large scale trials have been questioned and, certainly in forensic applications, they are essentially useless. There is an alternative which is not only simpler to understand, but also has much simpler mathematics when used practically. The mathematical derivation of the theory and formula remain complex, but in application it is easy and simple. This approach is called 'Bayesian statistics'. Although the title of this section is 'Old statistics and new statistics' this is slightly misleading. Bayesian statistics have become very powerful and widely used in recent years, but they originate with Reverend Thomas Bayes (1702–61), a Presbyterian minister. The key work was published by a friend of his in 1763. As an aside, the age of Bayes when he died can be used to demonstrate a false interpretation based on a simple statistical analysis. It is said, and widely believed, that during the Middle Ages life expectation was only 30 years. This is because of a lack of understanding of the way life expectancy is worked out using statistics. In the UK in 1948, life expectancy for males was 66.4 years and for females 71.2 years; at the end of the 20th century for men it was about 74.2 and for women 79.4 years. What this primarily reflects, but is not always realised, is that childhood is a very dangerous time. If you look in an ancient churchyard you will find that a lot of individuals lived for a very long time. To take the case of our Middle Ages example, if average life expectancy was 30 years, and mean age at death includes children, only 50% of whom survived, it would be reasonable to expect that if you made it past childhood you could expect to live until you were 60. If you want an average life expectancy you have to take everyone into account. So saying life expectancy was only 30 years is not the same as saying peopled only lived into their 30s.

With Bayesian statistics there is an element about it which does not always sit comfortably with traditional statistical calculations because it takes some notion of your belief before the data was available. This is termed the *prior probability*. The prior probabilities are then modified in light of the data, in the form of the *likelihood ratio*, to give the *posterior probability*. The one great advantage of this is that we really can say that a 95% confidence limit really is a 95% probability of finding that outcome, which cannot be done with classical statistics. We can therefore state simply that:

prior odds x likelihood ratio = posterior odds

It is of course the posterior odds in which we are interested, as this is what is presented to court. It is now in a form that can be easily understood. But we should consider the possibility of other information which could and should alter the prior odds. For example, if an individual is linked to an event by DNA evidence alone, it might be assumed that the individual was there and responsible for the event, but if he was seen, perhaps recorded on a security camera, many miles away, it will be necessary to review the prior odds and therefore the eventual outcome. If it is not possible for the individual to have got from the sighting to the event by the time it happened, the posterior odds shrink considerably. Indeed, if he was not there then no amount of DNA evidence can *prove* he was; an error must have taken place, or two people share the same DNA.

Having dealt with the Bayesian approach, the court must decide the value of prior evidence and therefore the value of the posterior evidence. It is most definitely the scientist who should influence this thinking. All a scientist can detail is the likelihood ratio, neither prior nor posterior odds. Such interpretation is for the court alone. So in the case above, where DNA evidence was found at a crime scene the scientist can only state the likelihood ratio of this coming from the individual; it is up to the court to decide that the other evidence, photographed at the same time miles away, for example, increases the prior odds to such a high level that the posterior odds are so small as to rule the accused out of the picture. Any assumption of prior odds by the scientist is both unscientific and would be making a legally wrong suggestion. The evidence of the scientist would be biased.

Expression of the likelihood ratio in forensic applications involving DNA evidence is quite simple and is usually no longer stated as a likelihood ratio but as a probability that one event is more likely than another. This is not to confuse the issue, but to make it easier for the court to understand the value of a result. I am not entirely convinced by this line of reasoning, but it is the way it is done. The way that DNA evidence is expressed is often further simplified in forensic science reports, as presented in court. This is stated as, say, one in 19,000,000 that a particular profile would be found by chance alone, with adjuncts such as:

> I have considered two propositions:
>
> - that the body fluid came from xxxxx;
> - that the body fluid came from an unknown person unrelated to xxxxx.
>
> If the STR profiles came from xxxxx, then I would expect the profiles to match.

At this point simplification can take a turn for the worse, almost patronising the jury in criminal cases or the judge in paternity disputes. The forensic scientist may then say that he has evaluated the significance of the findings according to the following scale: no; weak; moderate; moderately strong; strong; very strong; extremely strong support.

This evaluation is presumably aimed at addressing the idea that for most people very large numbers are almost impossible to visualise the meaning of.

When a probability is given, for example, of one in 100,000,000, trying to get a grip on the meaning of 100,000,000 is without doubt difficult. But it is surely incumbent on the court to decide whether this figure is extremely strong support for the proposition that a sample came from a specific individual, especially in light of other evidence which the forensic scientist cannot know; better then to simply state the likelihood ratio that the results were 100,000,000 more likely if they came from the specified individual than from an unrelated individual. We should not be afraid of big numbers, and no level of probability can rule out errors or surprises.

Hopefully the previous arguments have shown that it is possible to, in effect, deal with statistical probabilities intuitively, but caution has to be exercised because the assignment of 'prior odds' is very much a personal interpretation and so is the assessment of the likelihood ratio as relevant for any particular evidence of value.

If a juror thinks that a piece of evidence is valid as either incriminating or not, then the juror is deciding whether they assess a piece of evidence more likely if it fits either the prosecution or defence scenario. This is logically thinking the process through. Usually DNA evidence is seen as highly plausible, but it is not infallible.

5.3 Different questions for different cases

When a case appears, either involving criminal charges or a civil law suit, the first question that is asked will be 'is the accused guilty?' or 'is the named individual the father?'. These are in fact two completely different questions, but in the case of rape resulting in a pregnancy they may need to be combined for the help of clarification in court. It is these questions and hypotheses which will be explored in this chapter. It is important that all alternative hypotheses are explored.

It is essential that a witness dealing with DNA evidence, indeed with any forensic evidence, does not state, or even infer, that they can give a probability for an event having occurred. They can only give a *likelihood ratio*, and this will be explored in some detail as a concept. It is often not enough to have a set of two simple hypotheses such as 'the person is guilty' and 'the person is not guilty'; more often it will help the court if the hypotheses for and against are clearly formulated. So let us start with the simpler case of parentage disputes, which usually involve paternity rather than maternity disputes.

5.3.1 Disputes of parentage

There is a very good reason for saying that although this section deals with disputes of parentage, it is usually that of paternity which is important. It is true that occasionally there are cases in which a child may have been taken from a maternity ward and therefore determination of maternity is required, but it is usually only in such mix-ups, whether deliberate or accidental, that disputes arise. Probably the only other situation where it would be necessary to prove maternity is in cases of adoption or very confused family relationships.

As we have already described, mitochondrial DNA (mtDNA) is inherited maternally, so you, whatever your sex, will have the same mtDNA as your mother. This means that in those rare situations where a question of maternity is involved mtDNA is ideal. There are some other rare situations where mtDNA can be of particular value. One such question is determining whether a group of individuals, male and female, are siblings. It is important to remember that mtDNA is only inherited maternally, so even if the siblings, say two boys and two girls, all have different fathers, they will all have the same mtDNA as their mother and each other. This advantage is also a drawback: it means that in criminal cases mtDNA is of very limited value because not only do siblings all share the same mtDNA, but it runs largely unaltered through generations. This results in a current generation sharing the same mtDNA with their mother, her mother and all their maternal aunts and uncles, and all cousins who are children of their aunts, but not cousins who are children of their uncles. So to make use of mtDNA we have to be very clear as to what question it is we are asking and whether it will tell us anything if we do the analysis, or whether it will simply render 'empty' data, that is, yes, we get a result, but it does not clarify the situation in any way.

Except when mix-ups or an abduction have taken place, questions of maternity are not generally raised. Put bluntly, conception usually only has two present; birth usually involves more, and independent, observers to the mother / child relationship.

It has to be said, though, that family relationships can be far more complicated. Even before DNA profiles were available I was carrying out prenatal diagnosis tests which produced results that occasionally indicated that the husband was not the father. This, of course, results in a very difficult situation because prenatal diagnosis is not undertaken lightly – there is always a risk to the foetus. What has changed since then is that there are occasions when a mother will ask for a DNA test, sometimes when the child is a teenager, because she is unsure which partner is the father of her child. This doubt may linger for many years before action is taken and result in very difficult questions being asked which have to be addressed *before* any tests are carried out.

In terms of a client in your office, you have the same rights and duties of care as anyone, but you may find yourself put in an invidious position by being asked to determine which of two possible partners is the father of a child who may or may not be cogent of the nature of these tests. It should always be emphasised just how disruptive to a child it can be to be effectively forced to have a test that will determine a biological father: Dad is who you like, not who someone tells you is your father.

There are several different questions which can be framed when approaching a paternity dispute and, as we shall see, the questions can overlap with questions which arise from some criminal cases.

There are two basic questions which arise in paternity disputes, which are:

- Is there a suggested alternative father?
- Is there a completely unknown father?

The difference between these two questions is simple: the first question refers to a closed system, that is, there are only three adults and a child involved. This will arise in one of two broad ways. The first is if a couple with a child are faced with an individual who claims the child is his. In this case, it becomes straightforward to test the whole family and rule out one of the men as the father and the other as a possible candidate. Now, because there is no suggestion of a third party, the guarded tone of *possible candidate* can be taken in conjunction with this to declare the possible father as the father. The point to remember here is that any DNA evidence which gives an inclusion is not and never can be *absolute* on its own. Normally we would expect some sort of statement of probability, and indeed it may still be valid in this case to expect a statement such as 'individual X is 99% likely to be the father of child Y', but in this particular case that residual doubt is irrelevant.

The second situation in which a closed system paternity dispute can arise is when a mother does not know for certain which of two men is the father of her child. This situation can also bifurcate into a situation where all parties co-operate to determine the truth, which has the same outcome as our first example, but co-operation is not always possible. It must be remembered that the mother might want to find out *discretely* which of two lovers is the father of her child. It is not unknown for a mother to have doubts for several years after the birth of her child, having married or lived with one of the putative fathers. We are dealing here with powerful emotions and great care has to be exercised when dealing with these situations.

It is not unusual for a mother in this situation to want the test to be carried out in secret. Under these circumstances she may be able to arrange for a sample, such as plucked hairs, from the child and the person with whom she is living, but not from the other suggested father. The two possible results here would, in the mind of the mother, both give a complete picture. If the man with whom she is living has a 99% probability of being the father, then as far as she is concerned he is. If the same man is excluded as the father, then even though no sample has at this point been taken from the other man she will know that he is the father. This can be seen as an unethical method of conducting a paternity test and it would certainly not result in information which could be used in court, but it may rest a family ghost. It may also create a huge family problem. What I have found is that if the exact situation is talked through sensitively with the mother a degree of honesty can be achieved in which it can be seen that if the relationship is sound, knowing one way or the other would make no difference to her, but if it is not sound is it just an excuse to leave anyway? Either way what effect is it going to have on those who have been deceived? Very rarely can this sort of testing have a happy ending if it is discovered that testing has been carried out, regardless of the result.

Our second major question arises from paternity disputes where there is no alternative suggested father. Put another way, the suggestion is that person X is the father of child Y, a suggestion which is more accusation than not. This is the sort of situation most commonly found in paternity disputes. It is also the usual position in which the Child Support Agency finds itself concerned. Such cases as these are faced with an absolute necessity to be able to produce a probability of paternity. It does not matter exactly which type of DNA analysis is used; in probabilistic terms the result will range from 0, that is, complete exclusion, to as high a probability that it is possible to produce using the available technology. But however high this probability figure is, for example 99.999%, it can never give an *absolute* certainty of paternity; there is always a residual doubt.

A similar situation was found in a case which resulted in an exhumation. In situations where an individual dies leaving no will, or perhaps a controversial will, in which the estate is of great value, a child, or mother and child, may come forward with a claim on the estate. I have come across just such a case, where the deceased was buried before it was realised how valuable his estate was, at which point a woman came forward claiming the deceased was the father of her son. The following months resulted in an exhumation and a very difficult DNA analysis. It was difficult because DNA had to be extracted from bone marrow of the long bones without contamination of the final product. This had to be done using saws in a clean room. Eventually enough material was extracted to try a DNA analysis. The problem of determining paternity was compounded because, although DNA had been extracted, it was in such poor condition that only two partial profiles were produced. Luckily, comparison with mother and son showed that even the partial profile provided an exclusion of the deceased being the father. This does raise a particular point, however. When using short tandem repeat analysis for paternity testing, a large panel needs to be used, which is now the norm. The reason for this is that there is a fundamental difference between a scene of crime DNA sample and a paternity DNA sample. The difference is that during sperm production a process of cell division takes place called meiosis. The purpose of this is to reduce the number of chromosomes by half so that when the ovum is fertilised, which also has half the normal chromosome number, the full complement of chromosomes is restored. Because this process is complicated it is the point at which mutations take place, which can alter the number of repeats in an STR. This can result in a situation in which one STR appears to produce an exclusion of paternity.

Luckily mutation rates are relatively low so this does not happen very often. However, this is an area where there is some debate. At an international meeting in London in 2000 it was apparent that some testing laboratories would declare an absolute exclusion if they found one mismatched STR, but others would only do so if they found two or more mismatches. This difference is interesting but might be seen as missing the point if argued in court. If there is a mismatched STR, even if it is only one, it is impossible to determine whether it is a genuine indication of non-paternity or a mutation which has taken place. It could, along the same lines, be argued that two mismatched STRs could be the result of two independent mutations, even though this is very unlikely. As the number of paternity disputes resolved using this technology increases, so it becomes ever more likely that an individual will be excluded as the father of a child because two mismatched STRs rule him out, and yet he is actually the father. It is in this sort of situation where a statistical probability can help to clarify the position for the court, but unfortunately may also mislead the court: if a probability is given for a mutation event having taken place which is so large that the court assumes it could not have happened, and therefore assumes that an exclusion of paternity is demonstrated, and yet a mutation event has taken place, the accused is the father. In some cases the truth of paternity is going to be impossible to determine; only the two parents will know the truth, and sometimes with multiple partners even the mother my not know who the father is.

5.3.2 Criminal cases

For many men a paternity dispute is usually only a question of potential financial hardship, but for some it can be a cause of immense stress. For the mother, such questions range through such a wide area that it might encompass finance, stress, betrayal, dishonesty, desertion, and many such things. However, in criminal cases in which DNA analysis is used the result may be far more devastating.

It is axiomatic that we depend upon a benevolent society for the correct application of justice, but such things are historically delicate. If an aggressive parliament were to decide that the death penalty was appropriate in some cases, it could result in the death of an innocent: DNA cannot be the ultimate arbiter in such cases, even though this is the way that current trends are leading us, so great care needs to be exercised when interpreting DNA evidence.

Once a result has been prepared from a DNA sample the interpretation is crucial to the correct understanding of what the result means, and this interpretation revolves around how the results are expressed, which in turn depends upon which question is asked. This is where it becomes very easy to mislead with the wrong question and is often referred to as the 'prosecutor's fallacy'. This is not a new phenomenon, but has become rather more prominent in recent years because of the increasing use of DNA evidence. There are numerous practical examples which can be used to illustrate the prosecutor's fallacy, but it is probably best to stick to a strictly forensic analysis.

Once DNA evidence has been gathered in and results obtained, there are two different questions that can be asked if a match between an individual and a crime stain has been found. Remember that if an exclusion has been declared these questions are irrelevant – the individual could not possibly be responsible for the material recovered from a scene of crime. The two questions which arise from finding a match are:

(a) Given that the defendant is innocent what is the probability that the DNA profile from the defendant matches the profile which came from the crime scene?

(b) Given that the DNA profiles match from defendant and crime scene, what is the probability that the defendant is innocent?

It is obvious that that the first question relates to the evidence given by the expert witness, but it is the second question that the court is really interested in. The first question assumes innocence, while the second question assumes the DNA matches. The answer to these two questions can be radically different depending on all manner of information which the expert cannot give an opinion on. The expert can give an accurate assessment of the first question, and this is the only thing which a DNA expert can give an assessment of. Assuming that the work has been carried out correctly and the databases which are used for comparison are reliable, this is not an opinion but a statement of fact. So what you should see is either a *match probability* or a *likelihood ratio*. A match probability is a simple statement of the DNA profile being found at random in the population based upon comparison with a known and reliable database. This should be expressed as the probability that a particular individual, unrelated to the accused, will match the DNA profile of the crime sample, and in terms of numbers it is usual to express this as, say, 'one in 1,000,000'. Another way in which this can be expressed is as a likelihood ratio, in which case it would be expressed as 'the evidence obtained is 1,000,000 times more likely if the crime sample originated from the accused (or defendant)'.

The second question 'what is the probability that the defendant is innocent, given that his DNA profile matches the profile from the crime sample?' is not the same as the first question, and the answer to the first question can be radically different to the answer to this second question. The point here is that the answer to this second question is dependent in many ways upon the perception of the defendant's innocence, which is in itself a subjective appraisal of the situation.

To put this in perspective, an expert can give an accurate statistic of probability, but it is up to the court, or the jury, to decide that the defendant is or is not innocent regardless of the DNA result. After all, given a match between a crime sample and a defendant, if the defendant was a castrated eunuch it would be very difficult to conclude that the individual was responsible for a rape. So the answer to the first question is very different to the answer to the second question. The answer to the first question will remain the same, but in the case of perceptions of the honesty of a person this is a sliding scale and an expert cannot pass a comment on this, but it has regrettably happened in the case of *R v Deen* (1993) unreported, 21 December (CA), the first case where a conviction was based primarily on DNA evidence. The misunderstanding is now routinely called the 'prosecutor's fallacy' (*People v Collins* 66 California Reporter 497 (1968)).

The main problem with the prosecutor's fallacy is that although it is generally not stated explicitly, it can be simply stated as giving the answer to our second question as the answer to our first. In our example, the error would result in a statement to the affect that 'the probability that the accused is innocent, given the DNA evidence, is one in 1,000,000'. There is a very real problem with this in that the authority of an expert witness, whether prosecution or defence, can result in a statement of this type being believed completely, and of course, once stated it does not matter what the judge directs the jury to believe, the genie is out of the bottle and cannot be put back. Perhaps more difficult is the possibility that a jury may hear the correct and unbiased information from the expert, but takes the leap to the prosecutor's fallacy themselves. It has sometimes been said that it is essential that the jury should be given an explicit warning that the data as presented can only be interpreted in the manner stated by the forensic scientist. Here there is some room for debate. Psychologists tell us that if you say to an individual 'don't think about a pink elephant' a pink elephant is precisely what they *will* think about. So saying this is the only interpretation of the results which is permissible may result in the jury asking themselves 'what other way of interpreting them is there?'. It might be suggested, then, that two alternatives to this dilemma are possible. The first is not to say anything and hope, possibly not the best route. The second takes longer but might in the long run be better. Explain to the jury what the prosecutor's fallacy is and why such an interpretation must be avoided.

Such is the perceived power of DNA evidence and the weight given to scientific testimony that if it is not treated carefully and with enormous sensitivity it is possible that the jury will denigrate the other evidence in favour of an assumption that the match between DNA profiles from a crime scene and the accused prove guilt. It is not the job of the forensic scientist to present data which could be misinterpreted, only to help the jury with as an objective assessment of the data as is possible.

SUMMARY

We have seen in this chapter how important it is for the forensic scientist to know the type of sample which is being analysed so that the correct question can be answered. There is no point in asking questions about paternity in a criminal investigation with a scene of crime stain, and the converse is also true. The exact questions which are used, and the manner in which they are tested, is explained for criminal cases and paternity disputes where there is an alternative named father and cases where there is not.

The statistical interpretation of results has been looked at in some detail without recourse to formula. Much of the data presented in court that has originated from statistical analysis is relatively easy to understand if looked at in a common sense way, without being daunted by the numerical manipulations that have to be carried out to arrive at the final figure, as presented in court. Odds are discussed in contrast to probabilities ,and the possible reason why odds are not widely used, even though many people can intuitively manipulate odds but have trouble with probabilities. The precise and very limited questions that DNA analysis can and cannot answer have been explored, in conjunction with a close look at the prosecutor's fallacy. Great care should be exercised in framing the wording of results of analysis so as not to mislead the jury into thinking that the stated probability is the probability of guilt or innocence.

CHAPTER 6

DNA DATABASES

INTRODUCTION

There are many different ways in which DNA profiles can be assessed, but it is never enough to simply say that a match has been found between a crime stain and an individual and, therefore, this implies the crime stain originates from the accused. So the question arises: how do we assess the result of a match? The answer is the use of a database. There are broadly two different types of database: the first is used to calculate frequencies of DNA profile, and the second is used as a comparison between an anonymous crime sample and an arrested individual.

Both of these databases have two very different structures which we will look at in more detail. In general terms, a database is any collection of data in any form. In the context of a DNA database, the data can be stored in a number of ways depending on what type of analysis has been carried out. Early attempts at constructing a DNA database were extremely difficult because of the complexity of the result, and comparison between individuals was not easily carried out. What was possible was the calculation of the frequencies of bands in populations. Modern databases are far better because the results are presented numerically, and are therefore amenable to comparison between individuals as well as constructing frequency databases.

6.1 Types of databases and their ethical implications

In broad terms there are two forms of database which are completely different from each other:

- collections of anonymous data, used to generate frequencies for given profiles;
- named databases, so that a DNA crime sample can be compared with known individuals.

In this section, we will look at anonymous databases first as these are the most straightforward to understand and only create a few contentious issues. We should always remember that if a scene of crime sample and a sample from a suspect do not match we have an exclusion, and therefore no database matching needs to be carried out. If a scene of crime sample and a suspect's sample does match, then we need to know how likely it is that this profile will be found by chance alone. It is using an anonymous database that enables us to answer this question. With the gradual accumulation of DNA data some questions have already been asked, but even more are needed because the implications of these databases for us all are considerable.

The physical manifestation of a modern DNA database is prosaic to the point of dull: just a series of boxes in a computer room like any other computer room. This belies the content, probably the most powerful collection of personal data ever held: over 1,000,000 samples currently in the UK, and by 2004 it is hoped that every offender will be on the database: about 3.5 million samples. It has also been suggested that the Home Office would like a database of every single individual in the country. This may also involve the storage of samples – a sample database – which raises questions as to future uses of our DNA for purposes which we do not currently hold as valid. This attempt to change the rules so that samples taken from individuals later found innocent can be kept, both as samples and as profiles, is lamentable. It is not allowed in any other country in Europe or in the USA.

The retention of samples is an affront to justice if only because an acquitted person is still paying a price: that of later possibly being wrongly accused of another crime by a chance match with a crime scene sample. The harrowing and embarrassing event of arrest, and then having to justify your innocence, is not one to be relished, especially with the possibility of effects on such areas as employment. One of the motivations for the change in the law is the case of Michael Weir. He was picked up on drugs charges, later dropped when a mouth swab was taken. Instead of disposing of the sample it was kept, against all the rules. When a bungled burglary resulted in the death of a man, it was found that not all the blood came from the victim: it matched that of Weir. The conviction was appealed against on the basis of the DNA having been held unlawfully. When the Law Lords reviewed the case again, it was decided that the acquittal on appeal was contrary to good sense and it was wrong to exclude the DNA match because of the manner in which it had been found.

This entire debate about the construction of these databases has taken a step forward with the new plans that would allow, for example, all those tested to eliminate them from enquiries having their DNA profiles stored indefinitely, as would be the sample from the victim. Storage, it is said, would be linked to permission, but as we have seen above, permissions may be forgotten or not asked for. Currently the Data Protection Act 1998 allows for any volunteer who provides a sample to request that the sample and all associated records be destroyed. The suggested legislation would specifically remove this right, which is a bit mean because it is, after all, your DNA, no one else's. It should be noted that members of the police force are themselves somewhat reluctant to donate DNA for the database. The suggestion by Sir Alec Jeffreys cannot be gainsaid: the official perception of people who have been picked up having been suspected of an offence are more likely to be criminals, so keep their samples, you never know when they might be useful. This is no doubt never explicitly stated, but we must question the motivation. There seems to be little in the Human Rights Act 1998 which does not allow for the construction of these databases.

One more point about databases is that they tend to be shutting the stable door after the horse has bolted. There does not seem to be any reduction in violent crime, although there may be an increase in 'clear up' rate, just as societies that insist on the use of identity cards have just as much crime as societies of similar political structure that do not. Many people would prefer that it was not necessary to move into the dark and murky water of absolute DNA databases by dealing with the reasons the crimes are committed in the first place.

There is also a rather fanciful aspect to the retention of samples, or at least currently fanciful. There is a difference between what we know and what we would like to know. The forensic scientist, along with the police and other groups, would like to be able to say something about a person's appearance, not just their partial profile as is currently used. Such ideas include height, hair colour, eye colour, skin tone, or virtually anything that could be used to produce an image of the culprit. These ideas are based on the rather simple and incorrect idea that knowing the DNA base sequence of a gene will tell you how it works. This is simply not true, with interactions between genes, between gene products and between genes and products of other genes. The belief in the simplicity of genes and DNA sequences telling us all in a very straightforward way is due to a lack of understanding of genetics, which tells us that the few simple cases of Mendelian inheritance which we know are relatively unusual in the overall scheme of things.

6.1.1 Anonymous databases

It may seem a fairly straightforward activity to collect data in the form of DNA profiles so that the frequency of any given profile can be calculated, and therefore also the probability of finding the result by chance alone. Much has been written about this subject but it really comes down to a very few questions.

The first of these questions is: how easy is it to create a database in the first place? Well, this depends upon the type of DNA analysis which has been carried out. Some of the older methods of producing a DNA profile are intrinsically flawed as systems to produce a database which is reliable.

Consider the purchase of potatoes. We expect the weight to be measured accurately, but we can live with some variation, up or down, within a range which is acceptable to most people. What we would not accept is the use of a make-weight of a different vegetable. So with multilocus probes (MLPs) or single locus probes (SLPs) the general mass may be approximately calculated, but the truth is that if measurements are made over a mass range of about five kilobases, using gels to separate fragments just cannot identify accurately and precisely the exact mass of the DNA fragments which appear as bands in a profile. This means that such a database is a good estimate, but only an estimate, of the size of DNA bands. There are several questions which this creates, some of which cannot be answered and some of which can.

The most important question is: how accurate are such databases? If we can only say that a single locus or multilocus probe system gives an estimate of fragment mass, there is at least one question which can be asked which is of very great importance: how reliable are they? It is possible that although the mass measurement may appear to be the same, it is not possible to be certain that the base sequence of the DNA is identical, or that the mass measurement is identical. Measurement in these systems is subjective, even when automated. It is quite possible that even with the influence of forensic scientists on the perceived validity of these types of DNA profiles, it should be remembered that calculation of DNA mass on this scale can only ever be approximate, and DNA sequence differences are completely unknown. So if the mass of the bands is accepted as the same, that does not mean the base sequence is, in which case we can also say that there may well be some questionable convictions based on this technology. We should therefore regard this as a form of molecular Bertillonage: do not be bamboozled by technology; the questions which need to be asked are nearly always the same and the answers still have to be made not by forensic scientists but by geneticists who understand the biology of the system being tested. It has to be said that the question of whether we can absolutely rely on a database made up of MLP or SLP data is fundamentally unanswerable; it can only be stated that we can generate a rough guide to the frequencies of the different bands, and it is these 'different bands' which we should look at to understand how a database is constructed and used.

When we have an SLP or MLP profile, it is not the complete profile which is kept on the database, but the various individual bands which make up the profile. To try and create a database of complete profiles would be a virtual impossibility. The reason for this is quite simple. Consider this situation: in some cases using the entire profile a probability has been taken into court of one in 738,000,000,000,000 (Lander, ES, 'DNA fingerprinting on trial' (1989) 339 Nature 501–05). This completely meaningless figure is far too large to conceive of, and could not possibly be arrived at by simply trying to compare one entire profile with a database. To do such a thing would logically require that at least 738,000,000,000,000 profiles would have to be looked at to be able to say that this profile would only be found once. Since the figure quoted is so huge, it must be arrived at by a quite different route to make it a valid probability figure.

This is done not by looking at the complete profile, but on a band by band basis, and accumulating the probability by what is called the 'product rule'. This does, however, make for the need of some assumptions. The first of these is that two bands are not 'linked'. Linkage is an interesting biological phenomenon, often misrepresented and even more often misunderstood. If two genes are linked then they are on the same chromosome, but linkage studies refer to something rather more subtle: that is, the distance between genes on a chromosome. I have heard forensic scientists say that loci being tested are not linked, but they turn out to be on the same chromosome: *de facto* they are linked. However, the distance between them results in such a genetic reassortment of genes during reproduction that the linkage distance is so great that it would not be expected that gene A would be found with gene B more often than could be calculated using a relatively simple genetic model of inheritance. This problem of linkage is one which has to be very closely controlled if a database is going to make any sense at all. For example, if we calculate that the frequency of a band of a specific size can be said to be one in 10 and the frequency of another band is one in 20, we would expect to find these two together in only one out of 200 individuals. However, if these are closely linked we would then find that anything up to 50% could share the two bands, therefore making a mockery of the calculation of frequency based upon the idea that each band is inherited independently of every other band. So a primary consideration when compiling a database is to make sure that the different areas of the genome which is being tested are inherited independently of each other. This is pivotal no matter which sort of analysis is being used to form a database.

The current method of DNA profiling is short tandem repeat (STR) analysis, though this is likely to change over time as the technology becomes more sophisticated and the results easier to interpret and store. This is ideally suited to creation of a database because the process, as previously described, is mostly automated, which introduces a high level of precision into the results and at the same time the very nature of the technique also allows for a higher level of accuracy. Each tested STR is counted for a repeat number, so it is not a subjective assessment as to whether two bands match, but an objective numerical value. These STR values are sufficiently reliable for it to be possible over the very short sequences which are looked at to count down to a single base difference between samples.

So how are these databases constructed to give a useful picture of the frequency of a DNA profile? The method used is essentially the same regardless of the type of DNA profile produced, and is designed to produce a reliable snapshot of frequencies of different alleles, or STRs. For very rare alleles it may not be possible to estimate their frequency within a population because there are simply too few samples in the database. For most profiles this is not a problem. Although national and international databases proclaim that they may contain millions of entries, thereby giving them a sense of increased accuracy in their calculations, this is quite unnecessary. If a database is a true reflection of a population, after initial variation when only small numbers of samples were available, a reliable system will show progressively smaller and smaller changes to the frequency figures until they are essentially static. At this point, adding in new anonymous data will not change the picture for the forensic scientist. What would be of interest from a genetic point of view is if these databases continued to use the same method of data acquisition over centuries, which, it has to be said, is most unlikely, and the samples were date-tagged. This may then show us far more about the rate of mutation and, perhaps more importantly, the direction of mutation.

Once an anonymous database has been constructed it is necessary to extract some meaningful information from it, and this uses a process called the 'product rule', or sometimes the 'multiplication rule'. The product rule is based upon a major assumption: that the population does not contain sub-populations with distinct and different allele frequencies. Put another way, this requires the assumption to be made that any individual constitutes a set of alleles which can be seen as statistically independent selections from a common gene pool. As we will see later, this assumption can lead into murky waters if we are not very careful.

Given that our population is uniform, there are a series of steps which can be followed to create a DNA profile frequency. It is probably worth breaking this down into several steps for clarity:

(1) Find out what the frequency of the alleles are in a random sample of the population by counting the number of matching alleles. This does not require a theoretical model, as it is simply a counting process. The important aspect is to make sure that the population sample is large enough to cover as many of the alleles that are known to exist as is possible.

(2) Take the allele frequencies and use these to calculate the genotype frequency, that is, the frequency of the two alleles which we all carry: the genotype. This assumes that the two alleles are inherited independently from a mother or a father. In the case of the homozygote, this is calculated

by multiplying the allele frequency by itself. When it comes to heterozygotes, the calculation is very slightly different: we start by multiplying the allele frequencies together and then double the result. This is because there are two possible ways of ending up with the result: either the father can donate allele 1 and the mother allele 2, and vice versa. This can be expressed mathematically, but for the value of an explanation, this is not necessary. There is always a possibility in the case of a sample apparently homozygous – that is, with two alleles the same – that it is not actually homozygous, but for reasons of genetics there is only one allele present. This apparently unlikely situation is not so unlikely as one might imagine, given that small deletions of chromosomal material are really quite common.

(3) Calculate the frequency of the complete genotype. This is a simple process of multiplying all the genotype frequencies together. This must assume that there is no linkage between any of the alleles.

Using this method it is easy to see that even with a database of relatively modest size, it is possible to determine the probability of finding any given DNA profile. The result is that astronomical figures can be generated which are quite reliable, but seemingly ridiculous. The thinking on this works along the lines of 'if the frequency of this profile is less than the number of people in the world this profile should not exist'. As you can see, this is an argument which is back to front. We have the profile: what is the probability of finding the same by chance alone?

Once a database has been constructed of allele frequencies, when a match is found between profiles from a crime scene and an individual the above calculation can be used to calculate the probability of a chance match. But this depends upon another very significant assumption: that there is no population substructure.

Population substructure is not as contentious an issue as it was during the early development of DNA profiling, when it was simply not known what effect this would have on profiling results. In forensic terms, population substructures can be thought of as differences in allele frequencies which would result in a different frequency figure for a given profile between two or more populations. This operates on the principle that if a group carries characteristic allele frequencies, then knowing that one of these is carried infers membership of the group, which would alter the statistical expectation of finding other characteristic alleles, therefore the genotype frequency would be higher than expected using a simple calculation from a general database.

Interestingly the original arguments regarding population substructures stemmed from the observation that there really are large difference between some ethnic groups when protein polymorphisms or genetic diseases are looked at. However, these radical differences are of biological significance, reflecting evolutionary pressure exercised through environmental differences in origins. The important point here is that these are differences of biological significance, which, since we are looking at systems based on expressed gene sequences, should not be a surprise. But when we look at STR sequences it would be more of a surprise if these sequences were so variable because they have generally been regarded as 'junk' DNA; a better term would be non-coding DNA. This is a rather over-simple attitude towards STRs. There are a number of reasons for saying this. The first is that if we take out all the non-coding sequences from some genes, instead of making the gene more efficient it reduces expression.

Another reason that these sequences may not be 'junk' is that it has become increasingly apparent that it is not just the base sequence of DNA which is important to the expression of a gene – there is far more to genetics than that. One aspect becoming increasingly important is the physical position of the gene within the nucleus, and this is most likely controlled by repeat sequences. So not junk, really quite important: just not coding for a specific product.

So we should not be so surprised if the variation between populations when looking at STR profiles is far less than proteins or genetic diseases. This is more or less what we find. There are variations, but except when looking at extremely remote populations, the variations tend to be small. Even so, many studies have been carried out on different populations to clarify whether variations in STRs are significant when using databases. One result of this is that there is now a tendency to quote the most conservative probability value when taking results into court. This results in expressions of probability which tend to be in favour of the defendant, but this does not necessarily mean that it helps the defendant. The probabilities are now of such significance that even the most conservative values are enormous. It should also be realised that with every new STR that is used – now frequently more than 10 different STRs are used as against the original four – the overall measure of population substructure affecting the statistical analysis will reduce. This is because with some STRs one particular population may be different to others, but with other STRs different populations will vary, so the overall picture should become more uniform.

There are ways in which these databases can be compromised. One way that this might happen is by an individual being present on the database more than once, thereby skewing the frequency of the different alleles in the profile. If a single database is constructed from all samples, regardless of ethnicity, this will also have the tendency to alter the frequency of alleles by under- or over-representing various groups. This is easily remedied by separating the different ethnic groups into distinct databases. These only need to be very broad groupings because, contrary to popular belief, there are very few, if any, distinct racial groups which can be distinguished using STR technology. This is not really any surprise, because even isolated aboriginal tribes would have shared a common ancestor with the rest of humanity and so there are only two ways in which they could turn out to be unique in their profiles. The first is called the 'founder effect'. This describes a population arising from a very small number of individuals who do not carry the complete range of genetic variation found in the wider gene pool. The second is called 'genetic drift': a process in which random fluctuations take place in the frequency of alleles. This theoretically takes place in all populations, but it is only significant in small groups where, say, the only carrier of a particular allele dies, thereby eliminating that allele from the small gene pool.

At the other end of the spectrum, we can use well documented histories to show that overall there should be no substructuring of populations. For example, if we take the British, it is well documented historically that there has been a continuous influx of difference nationalities, from Romans, Vikings, Normans, Hugenots, European Jews through all sorts of different groups, up to the present day. Assimilation of these different groups not only enriches the language and names, but also renders it meaningless to try and distinguish a 'Briton' from the rest of Europe – we are all mongrels now.

6.1.2 Databases of named individuals

Given that we can calculate the probability of finding a profile by chance alone, this is very often enough information to take into court. But recent developments have resulted in another form of database which is not uniformally greeted with open arms. This is the database of named individuals. When an individual is arrested for an offence a sample is routinely taken, so although arrest may be for one particular offence, comparison with a database can be used in two ways to clarify the position. The first is if we have an arrested individual, a sample from whom can be used to compare with a crime scene database. This routinely occurs and has been used on many occasions to tie individuals arrested for one crime to one or more other crimes. This speeds up the process of crime solving quite considerably. When such a match to a crime sample is made a new sample is taken from the individual, the results of which can then be assessed in the usual manner and the results taken into court.

The other aspect of these types of database is the converse of the above case. When samples are taken from arrested and then convicted individuals, these are stored by name so that, should the same individual leave a sample suitable for DNA analysis at a crime scene, the sample can be analysed and a match found which puts a possible name to the originator of the crime sample.

This process has to be approached with some caution, however, because simple logic tells us that the more complete profiles we have in our database, the more likely it is that we will find a match. Even more, as the database of profiles increases we may start finding several matches. Consequently it is important that we do not rely only on such evidence. Such is the perceived power of DNA evidence that it may be believed despite evidence to the contrary which is far more compelling, such as the impossibility of an individual being at the scene of a crime. This random matching of a crime scene profile and the profile of an individual is one reason that can be cited for not having a national database of all individuals resident in a country, whether it is this one or any other. One reason for saying this is quite straightforward and not due to an unrealistic perception of what might happen. If a match was found between you, the reader, and a crime sample from a rape, the police would be duty-bound to investigate. Besides the intrinsic embarrassment of being questioned by the police in such a matter, it is entirely possible that you may have been at home on your own, or working late, making it impossible for you to provide an unassailable account of yourself. The only evidence is a DNA match, so should we rely only upon such evidence, no matter how compelling the result is? This also revises the public perception of how justice works. Under these circumstances it is no longer enough to say that the prosecution has to prove guilt, because the onus is now upon the defendant to discredit DNA evidence. The other reason for disputing the value of keeping such universal data is that it depends upon a belief in a benign state. Just as living memory shows that in Europe alone the benign state has waxed and waned, there is no intrinsic reason that super-surveillance of this sort might not be storing up problems for future generations, not us or perhaps even our grandchildren, but in the future, because we had lived in a benign state and thought that it would always be so.

Considering these ideas and facts we can see that there are a number of potential problems with databases. These are usually problems of logic, but it is always incumbent upon the advocate to take these into consideration when presented with DNA evidence utilising databases of any sort. If presented with a statement of a match, this does not mean that the matched person was responsible for the crime stain. In fact, we would expect that the number of matches would be calculable as the number of individuals on the databases multiplied by the expected frequency of the complete profile. But it should always be remembered that just because the probability of finding a random match is one in 1,000,000 this does not mean that the first, second or 100th profile tested will not produce a match: one in 1,000,000 does not mean that you will have to look at 1,000,000 samples to find a match.

Bearing in mind these arguments, another important aspect of DNA database searching is one that should not be influenced by time or cost now that computer searches are the only way in which profile comparisons are made. This is important because, by the very nature of coincidence and probability, finding a match should not stop the search across a database for other matches. If a premature stop was made it would not be possible to say anything about the result because it would not be certain whether all similar profiles had been found. This is an interesting philosophical question, because it produces the question 'can we ever rely upon a database if a single individual within a population has not been tested?'. So we come back, not to questions regarding the validity of the science or the chain of custody, which are easy to criticise, but to something more important.

It is too easy to say that we can prove a point: in truth we can only give weight to an argument in favour of our position. What DNA analysis does when carried out correctly is give weight to any other evidence there may be available. But conversely, when identification is taken from a database the other evidence may be such that no matter how much credence is given to the DNA result, the identified person could not be responsible. An example of such a dispute has arisen with the exhumation of James Hanratty. DNA evidence is said to support his conviction for murder, but a long term campaigner for the innocence of Hanratty, Paul Foot, states his position clearly when referring to his belief in Hanratty's innocence: '... if the DNA suggests otherwise, there must be something wrong with the DNA.' This is a conflict with no easy solution, possibly no solution at all: a simple stalemate of ideas.

This is particularly important in DNA analysis, where sometimes the wrong questions are asked. The primary case of this type is epitomised by the very reasonable expectation of the court to have an answer to the question 'how much do the results of DNA analysis increase the probability that the accused was responsible?'. What the DNA results actually tell us is the *probability* of finding this match by chance alone.

With these interpretations there comes another set of questions which are broadly 'what can you reasonably expect from an expert witness?'. The answer to this question is much the same in whatever discipline the expert works, but here we will confine ourselves to DNA.

6.2 Expert evidence in court

It has been debated as to whether an expert witness gives evidence of fact or opinion. Generally, though, there is a simple way of deciding this. Opinion is what one thinks, or a judgment based on grounds short of proof. But what an expert takes into court is a result which is based upon a recognised series of scientific activities and calculations. Such laboratory skills and theoretical knowledge as is required for DNA analysis is in the public domain: that is, it is open to anyone to gain and utilise this information. Of course, for the very practical reasons of time and effort this might not be practicable and therefore specialists are called upon to fill in the gaps. In some ways this is contradicted by simple observation of events. If in a case involving DNA two experts disagree, then there must be some element of opinion in one or both of them, otherwise the same facts would result in the same conclusions. This reflects the very nature of science: given a set of observations, two scientists may come to two different conclusions. What we would then do is take the two interpretations of the results and, using them, make a prediction as to the outcome of another related experiment. The interpretation which comes closest to predicting the outcome of the experiment is regarded as the one most likely to be correct, but it may still undergo considerable change and refinement as more information arises. In forensic cases this normal process is somewhat by-passed

The definition of an expert may be open to dispute, but what has been accepted for many years is that it is irrelevant as to how an expert has gained the necessary knowledge to be regarded as expert, only that it is demonstrable to the court that the expert is truly that (*R v Silverlock* [1894] QB 766). In the case of DNA experts the demonstration of expertise is usually based upon academic qualifications, with the proviso that the court is not particularly interested in what the expert has done, so much as whether the expert can add anything to the case which the court is hearing (*R v Oakley* (1980) 70 Cr App R 7). This addition to the information given to the court also depends upon the clarity of expression which the expert brings to the case. It was during the 18th century that experts started to play their modern role, as laid down by Lord Mansfield in 1782: the opinion of scientific men upon proven facts may be given by men of science within their own science (*Folkes v Chard* (1782) 3 Doug KB 157). That it was the 18th century that marked the start of the cult of the expert should be no surprise; the previous century had seen considerable change, from the science of Hooke and Newton to John Harrison's production of timepieces allowing the measurement of longitude and the change of the start of the year to 1 January in 1751.

Over the intervening years a great deal has been written regarding the necessity for an expert to be absolutely independent of the source of their funding. Even though an expert may be retained by one side of the case, the aim is to clarify the evidence for the court. Should anything transpire that alters the probative value of DNA evidence, it is incumbent upon the expert to alter the opinion as produced in a report or publicly in court. It is, after all, in everyone's interest to find the true perpetrator of a crime, and in the past the crimes involving DNA analysis have been of the most unpleasant kind: murder and rape. Now the net has been spread wider: traces containing DNA found at burglaries, DNA taken from the licked flap of an envelope or stamp from a poison pen letter, but as far as the expert is concerned every analysis is as important as any other. On this basis it is incumbent on the lawyers instructing an expert not to try and coach him in what he should say in court. Similarly, no attempt should be made to influence the structure or content of a report generated by an expert. You employ an expert specifically because the witness is peritus, expert, so they should be trusted to approach an analysis in an objective manner, and if counsel thinks they are not up to the job they should instruct another expert.

SUMMARY

This chapter has dealt with some apparently unconnected aspects of forensic DNA analysis. We started by looking at databases: what they are and how they are constructed. Besides this we also dealt with the different types of databases, from a collection of any sort of connected data to the anonymous and named individual databases that are currently in use. Within the context of DNA databases we looked at the way in which data is collected and the storage of samples. Also within the context of forensic databases, the potential problems of population substructures was investigated and the way in which such problems can be overcome, and also why the gradual movement of people around the globe is blurring the population substructure. If we look at variation in proteins, there are substructures which can be demonstrated. When we look at current methods of DNA profiling the techniques used look at non-coding regions which, from a genetic point of view, we would expect to vary from population to population in a similar way, the measurable variation reflecting the genetic distance, that is, time, between divergence of populations.

Carrying on from database construction, questions were raised about the ethics of these databases and the assumption that we now live in a benign society and will in the future, a proposition which cannot be justified by a review of recent history. These questions of ethical collection of data have been thrown into stark relief with the events of 11 September 2001, when terrorists destroyed the twin towers of the World Trade Centre in New York. The knee-jerk reaction is to instigate identity cards and complete DNA databases of all citizens. As we have seen, this may aid detection of the perpetrators, but may not stop the event in the first place. The second area which we looked at is related to these questions of ethics: the place of the expert witness in court, the history starting in the 18th century. We show the importance of the court seeing, and believing, that an expert does not work for the benefit of either the prosecution or defence: they work for the court and aim to help as much as is possible.

CHAPTER 7

ETHICAL CONSIDERATIONS OF DNA AND DNA PROFILING

INTRODUCTION

We touched on the ethical considerations of databases in Chapter 6, but here it would be worth looking at the whole question of DNA profiling and the ethical questions which really should be addressed as soon as possible. Genetics and DNA technology in general have thrown up questions which could not even be imagined half a century ago. It has also put biological science as a whole into the same arena as chemistry and physics. That is to say, chemistry and physics started their ethical and moral questioning centuries before when they came into direct conflict with the Church, later it was as moral transgressors within the realms of pollution and weaponry that caused such distrust. Biology on the other hand had always been seen as both a 'soft', or easy, science and one which was on the side of the 'natural' world. The inverted commas are deliberate because much of what we think of as natural is in fact man made, especially in the environment.

Now the situation has changed, this is partly due to the increasing public unease of animals in medical research, but especially in the wake of the destruction of the World Trade Centre in New York on 11 September 2001 and the subsequent sending of anthrax spores through the post which resulted in the death of postal workers. Biology is now perceived as just as ripe for moral questioning as any other science, and it should be remembered that although current uses of DNA which involve the courts may well expand in the next few years as challenges are mounted in all manner of cases.

7.1 What are the ethical questions and considerations concerning DNA?

When it comes to DNA and ethics, virtually any question that can be imagined will at some time have been asked and there are some not even thought of yet which will have to addressed in the future. Although we will look at specific questions later, here it would be useful to look at general ideas of ethical questions.

It is easy to imagine that ethical, or moral, questions regarding personal relationships within a community have not changed a great deal since philosophy emerged as a subject in its own right. However, relationships between individuals and the State have changed beyond recognition from the time when the Greek philosopher Eudoxus coined the aphorism 'Pleasure is the supreme good'. Such statements are common place amongst essentially agrarian trading nations. On the other side of the world Lao Tzu said in about 550BC 'One who exalts in the killing of men will never have his way in the empire'. These are very laudable ideas and have a place in any general system of ethical thought, but it is also important to remember that this, like so many other areas of generalisation may not be able to deal with the very specific questions which arise in a very intricate and technical society. It is probably because of this that many questions, the checks and balances, which should have been asked before the introduction of some new technology were not. Think of it in another way, trying to frame up general questions to cover all eventualities will not work when there are so many conflicting interests at stake.

Without a specific idea of the sorts of ethical questions we would like answered we are working in the dark. Unfortunately philosophers and theoreticians who study ethics tend not to deal in specifics, but try and formulate rules and frameworks of thought which can then be adapted to specific questions. This may seem a rather soft approach, but it has the merit of being able to at least help in answering, if not actually answering, a question in the future which was not even dreamt of when the theoretical consideration of ethics started.

Stevenson, in *Ethics and Language* (1944, Michigan: University of Michigan), tried to demonstrate that ethics can be a rational discourse, by saying that if an individual says that tolerance is good the individual is approving of tolerance, but also more significantly, suggesting that you do as well. If you do not, then you have to be persuaded. But that implies a value judgement on the arguments which are to be put to persuade you that tolerance is good. The idea of persuasion is an interesting one, because the philosopher is always trying to produce an algebraic description of ethics and morals. The other end of the spectrum is the case where it could be stated that what is true in one case, or held to be true by an individual in a particular case, must be true in all other cases.

One could logically see that this latter case would result in a pacifist point of view, that is, it is not right to kill so I will not kill. A general philosophical idea of ethics taken as a personal guide. Where this and every other argument falls down is in cases where a terrorist says it is correct for me to kill, but not for you. Such moral conundrums have stretched moral debate since the dawn of rational thought, with solutions being found in every moral and ethical document, whether religious or secular. But where does this lead us in terms of the legal aspects of the application of DNA technology? In a way into a more complicated world, but also one far more relevant to the individual than a theoretical argument. DNA profiling affects the individual far more than any aspect of the other sciences. Physics has never singled out an individual, like chemistry the moral repercussions these sciences have wrought have been on a grander scale. You may be a victim, but you are not alone. This will be small comfort to the victim, but there is solidarity in social cohesion. DNA is different, it can be used not only to single out the individual, but also to penalise and degrade that individual.

The first thing to be said about ethical questions is a very practical one. It assumes a benign State, a regime which is trying to do the best for the population as a whole. A tyrannical regime of any sort can do what it likes and therefore does not have to be morally accountable for its actions. This point is important because in a benign State it is everyone's right, if not duty, to challenge morally repugnant actions. In such a State it is legal action which is the immediate point of challenge to such behaviour, whether it is an individual committing a crime, which we have collectively decided is not acceptable, or a government behaving in a manner which a social group or individual thinks is wrong. So the first port of call will be the courts, where we should be able to expect an independent judiciary.

However, it is also true that sometimes actions and decisions are taken which although in themselves not contentious, accumulate along with other legislation to create a highly questionable situation. Note here that the situation becomes questionable, an interpretation of the rules becomes possible which some would simply not agree with. For example, progressive attitudes towards free speech has resulted in the situation being taken advantage of by extreme groups for political ends.

7.2 Cloning as a legal issue

It is also true that scientific developments have taken place which throw up new possibilities which, rightly or wrongly, were not foreseen and cause consternation amongst the public and legislators alike. A case here would be the cloning of Dolly the sheep. This was the first cloning of an adult sheep, but although everyone seemed surprised by this it did not happen out of the blue. It should have been realised that this was going to take place long before because not only had the research been running for several years, but the year before Dolly was born the same group had cloned Morag and Megan, but the difference was that these two sheep were cloned not from an adult but from an already fertilised egg. Very few results of this magnitude arrive without warning. The result of Dolly was primarily one of throwing up questions which needed to be debated before the cloning took place, not afterwards. A good example of ignoring such notions as pre-empting ethical problems before they arise can be seen in the problems associated with human cloning.

At the end of 2001 a legal challenge was mounted by the Pro-Life Alliance to the system of licensing the production of human clones for therapeutic reasons instituted by the government. The argument demonstrated a loop hole in the current legislation covering human cloning. The case was heard at the High Court and was based upon the definition of an embryo which had been produced by cell nuclear transfer, the method used to produce Dolly the sheep. This involves fusion of the nucleus from a mature cell with an egg which has had its nucleus removed. The important point here is that no act of fertilisation is involved and it is on this point that the arguments were made.

The original Human Fertilisation and Embryology Act 1990 was amended in 2000 so that cloned embryos were covered, but the definition of an embryo, that is a fertilised egg, was not altered. Since a cloned embryo has not undergone fertilisation it is not in fact covered by the Act. So although a contradiction in terms, for the purpose of the law a cloned embryo is not an embryo.

The outcome of which was that the High Court decided that the licensing arrangements for embryo cloning did not hold for implantation of cloned embryos, all of a sudden it became apparent that producing an infant from a cloned adult cell was not ruled out. This legislative anomaly was that it should never have been exposed by a court ruling, it should have been dealt with by Parliament long ago. When Dolly the sheep was born in 1997 it was immediately obvious that sex may not be the only way to produce new offspring. In the USA the government quickly took this on board and revised their own definition of an embryo. In the UK the committee of MPs dealing with science and technology warned the government of the potential problems this definition of an embryo might cause. On Friday 18 January 2002, Master of Rolls, Lord Phillips of Worth Matravers, sitting with two other judges, said that an embryo created by cloning did fall within the legal definition of an embryo, even though no fertilisation had taken place. This finally brought human cloning in the UK for medical research into the Human Fertilisation and Embryology Act 1990.

Whether you agree or disagree with the principles involved there are many questions which are raised. Broadly speaking there are two types of cloning in use here, one is cloning fertilised embryo cells and the other is cloning of other cells. But what is the difference? If nature can, and does, produce complete individuals from a single cell, then at what point do we say that cloning a cell is tantamount to usurping the position of nature. But it is the very nature of human curiosity to try and understand the world about us, including how it is that we cannot artificially create a viable organism. Put bluntly, if it happens in nature, why can't we do it?

This debate is complicated because identical twins can be seen as clones of each other. Although semantic debates in themselves can be interesting it would at this stage be worth considering what we mean by 'clone' and why it results in some very specific grammar. A clone is any group of cells, which includes a complete organism, which derives from a single progenitor cell. So Dolly the sheep is a clone of her mother, cloned from a cell of her mother. Identical twins are clones of each other from an original ovum. So not only do we clone by accident, in the case of identical twins, but for at least the last half century we have been cloning human cells deliberately and this deliberate cloning has been done in the quest for methods of prenatal diagnostics.

When foetal cells are removed so that they can be tested for large scale genetic defects, such as Down's syndrome and other conditions not compatible with life, the cells are routinely grown before the testing is carried out. Each group of cells is a clone of the first one which started dividing, each clone has the entire genetic content of the foetus from which it originated, but no one would suggest that there is sentience or soul present. Many of the samples of cloned cells are then frozen and stored, such that they can be defrosted and grown on again later. This is cloning and storage of human cells in exactly the same way that cloning and storage of human embryos is, in many ways they are separated by a distinction without a difference and I would not like to be the person that had to tell a seriously, or even terminally, ill individual that it is not possible to treat them because the only way is to produce immunologically sound material which they will not reject by cloning – and that this is not allowed. It was decided on 15 November 2001 that cloning of embryos for therapeutic research should no longer be licensed. But cloning one for birth apparently is and there are medical practitioners who seem to think that this is a good and practical idea. It is suspected that the incredibly high failure rate of cloned foetuses will mitigate against pursuing human clones. To put numbers on this, of 277 attempts only one sheep, Dolly, was borne and further successful examples of animal cloning have been just as hard won. But failure in this context is not a simple, clear, non-viable embryo, it includes gross malformations and developmental problems. These would not be an acceptable outcome in human cloning.

This problem of not thinking about questions on a 'what if?' basis before the practical necessity arises is exactly the same situation that seems to have occurred with DNA profiling and genetic testing for disease genes. We have simply not been ready as a society to address questions which are going to have profound affects for future generations.

This, sadly, is a general failing. Statements such as 'think of the children', have very little power to motivate; what does motivate seems to be political will and commerce. It is true, as discussed earlier, that large numbers are not easily conceived of. What is also true is that long periods of time are not easily comprehended either. So, to take an example from a different science, but one which is very real now and can therefore give us pointers to the future of our ethical problems in genetics, let us consider the question of nuclear waste. We can visualise this not just as a physical problem but an ethical one which is dependent upon society and the good will of society as well.

The long term control of nuclear waste is a problem. No matter how it is stored or dealt with it needs to be looked after for a very long time. Given the half-life of some of this material – that is the length of time it takes to reduce its radioactivity by half – the storage times are prodigiously long. It is not unrealistic to say that storage should be in excess of 10,000 years. But no civilisation has been around that long and it would require a great leap of faith to suggest that the current nuclear powers would remain intact, politically stable and financially able to look after such a potential problem for so long.

It is to be hoped that humanity is going to out-last nuclear waste, but the questions regarding political stability remain. We simply do not know what sort of a government we will have 1,000 years hence, we do not know what sort of data they will hold about our genes, so now is the time to question their perceived right to hold such information. Now is the time to challenge the perceived right of testers to take samples and find out whatever they like about an individual and possibly pass it on.

7.3 Insurance and genetics

What we are talking about here is a type of right to privacy that has never been tested before. The right to deny any access to your genetic data. If we do not have that then we become public property. It should not be forgotten that taking a sample and testing it does not actually destroy the sample, it can be stored and used later for further tests as the technology develops. Here I do not mean just criminal samples for inclusion on a database, but samples which can be used later for determination of potential medical conditions and the information passed to a third party. This is not so far fetched even now. The Home Office did state that no criminal profiling would use areas of the genome which could result in a diagnostic test being made inadvertently. Unfortunately, they do not have the expertise to be so certain about these tests which they carry out. They store data which is becoming increasingly more complex, one day an insurance company will make them an offer for it and then the real social problems will start. This may be next year or 500 years from now, but I and many others are sure it will take place, unless we challenge the assumptions which are being made now. These assumptions come in a number of different ways, but are generally self-explanatory:

- That a government will remain a benign state that looks after the benefits of the individual in society.
- That data taken for one purpose is not passed on to another department for other uses.
- No data should be passed to a commercial company.

These are ideas which are quite reasonable, but which cannot be guaranteed in perpetuity for many different reasons, not least of which is that we cannot foresee the future.

The best way in which we can help future generations therefore, probably the only way, is to have a judiciary which is both willing and able to confront difficult questions before they need to be answered. In practical terms this would equate to entering into the debate as to the amount of genetic data which any government department should be allowed to collect. It should not be imagined that these questions only affect the current generation, that is the one extant at any given time, because building up a picture of the genetic composition of a population has far more repercussions than that.

If data was to be collected now which indicated what the ethnic origin of a sample was, we might be quite happy with this in the certain knowledge that it would not be misused. But certain knowledge is in fact shifting sands, there can be no certainty about future social and political systems which might just decide that their plan for ethnic cleansing would be easier if genetic data on ethnic origin could be used to separate group A from group B. It is not just this sort of information which should be questioned and neither is it so far into the future when we will all be put at a disadvantage unless a challenge is made to the use of genetic data by those not able to assess it properly.

An increasing concern amongst geneticists is epidemiological data, as well as personal data, which is then used by insurance companies. This is an immense source of concern for several reasons, but before looking at the reasons for our concern, it would be well to look at the mode of inheritance which many of these genetic disorders follow.

Those genetic conditions of which the public are most aware are often inherited in a relatively straightforward way. Among these we can count cystic fibrosis, sickle cell anaemia, Huntington's chorea and Duchenne muscular dystrophy. The most straight forward inherited condition of these are cystic fibrosis and sickle cell anaemia, you can be an unaffected carrier with one defective gene, but one perfectly normal one which functions correctly and that is all you need. If you should marry another carrier however, simple patterns of inheritance indicate that the probability of producing an affected child is one in four, the probability of producing a non-carrier child is also one in four. The probability of producing a carrier child is one in two, or 50%. This is a probability, nothing more, so who should have access?

When it comes to Huntington's chorea the situation starts to become a little cloudy, and, with further examples which we shall look at, will become very difficult to interpret. Huntington's chorea is generally considered to be a dominantly inherited condition. But wait, why do the onset of symptoms occur at different times of life and with different rates of progression? Surely this means that it is not just a case of dominant/recessive, but if it was, then it would be easy to define the mode of inheritance. But it is not so easy, even in this case where we can say with certainty that an individual does or does not carry the gene and therefore will or will not have the disease, we are still unable to say when the disease will manifest itself. When it comes to other forms of inheritance the story becomes ever more complicated and the questions which need to be addressed ever more convoluted. A very good example of this is found in breast cancer. It is known that breast cancer is associated with a gene called BRCA1. About 5% of breast cancers are the result of this gene, and about 70% of those women who carry the gene will die as a result before they are 70 years old. But of course, that leaves us with 30% of carriers who never succumb to the disease. So the question is simple, what protects the lucky 30%? This is unknown and there is no way of predicting if a BRCA1 carrier is in the 70% or 30%. So it is here that the ethical consideration comes in and possibly the legal challenge.

Should an insurance company be able to either insist either on an individual having a test, or having had the test voluntarily, be able to insist on seeing the results? I do not think so. No matter what the Association of British

Insurers say, their logic is fundamentally flawed. There are two basic reasons for saying this, but it would be well first to look at the manner in which insurance works.

When calculating insurance premiums, there are two basic ways in which it is done. The first is called mutuality. This keeps all the people at the same risk together and therefore sharing the costs, consequently an insurance company would like lots of low risk people to maximise profits. This is the situation generally used in America where health insurance for some individuals can be impossible to find because they are perceived to be in a high risk group. The method normally found in the UK is, at the moment, slightly different. This system is called solidarity, everyone shares the cost of insurance, across the entire gamut of risk. Even so, there have been modifiers which have crept in, like smoking or obesity. In the case of smoking it is a self-inflicted injury, and for the most part so is obesity, but not always. Generally speaking, genetic information can be ignored using this model.

So we return to our original supposition, why not test everyone and modify their premiums accordingly, which is what the insurance industry would like? Well, to begin with this would be a 'cherry picking' exercise, what ever is said it can be assumed that the truth, now or later, is that if insurance companies were allowed to assess individual risk someone would end up as uninsurable, while those that probably do not need insurance will be quite happily given it. So if the claim is that there is no intention to increase profits, which it has been stated to be, why bother? Is it altruism on the part of insurance companies to put premiums up for one group and down for another? This brings us to point two. If there is no desire to increase profits, why not retain the actuarial system currently in place? Actuarial tables have been used for centuries and give a good guide to the numbers of any age cohort who will die at any given time. This system works for both the insured and the insurer, to change it is to load the dice in a game of chance in favour of the dice holder. The insurers want to bet on a certainty, the rest of us want access to affordable insurance.

This is the point where the legal challenge should be pursued. Discrimination in any form is both undesirable and dangerous. It is undesirable because we may lose a significant resource in the shape of our genetic diversity. After all, we have seen that some genes which are routinely described as 'disease genes' have turned out to confer additional fitness to the unaffected carriers, such as sickle cell anaemia (malaria resistance) and cystic fibrosis (tuberculosis resistance). It is also dangerous because we cannot tell what path this sort of action could lead us down, eugenics is not a very sensible route for humanity to take. A primary concern in this sort of testing is that the individuals that are making judgements on the results of these tests are simply not capable of making them. With any genetic test counselling is essential, without it the misery which can be caused within a family can be immense. Such things should be challenged before the situation becomes uncontrollable.

During the Human Genome Project it was discovered that in excess of 1.4 million single nucleotide polymorphisms (SNPs) are present in the human genome. Many of these are of considerable importance in testing for specific genetic conditions, even down to such things as adverse reactions to specific drugs. This will be of enormous benefit because although an adverse reaction may be a simple headache or weight loss, they can be so severe as to result in death. But SNPs have another practical application in the Criminal Justice system. They can be used in large panels to produce a DNA profile for identification. But even now it is reported that an American company, DNAPrint Genomics in Florida is patenting a test which tests for SNPs which correlate with eye colour. They are not trying to determine eye colour by looking at the genes which actually code for eye colour in their entirety, but at single bases differences which indicate the type of gene present and therefore the probable colour of the eye. A test of this type may be available shortly since eye colour is a genetically determined trait, but more fanciful ideas of testing in the same way for height and weight are less likely to reach fruition because of the very high environmental element in these two. This example is a taste of the future. Perhaps individuals and society as a whole will not mind this sort of information being collected, but I would have grave misgivings about collection of such information. Once such tests are available any unscrupulous regime could start eugenics programmes on very spurious grounds, but justifying it with application of a scientific test.

The use of SNPs forensically is also likely to run into problems if for some reason the ones chosen for criminal investigations turn out later to reveal information about an individuals health in some way. This may be quite subtle, such as potential for heart disease. If the test has been made and this information is a by-product of the test the question needs to asked as to whether it should have been done in the first place and secondly whether the tested individual should be told. They may not want to know, but if the testing authority has information which might be used to improve the health of an individual does it have a duty to pass this on? Or would the tested individual have the right to say that they have been tested for a medical condition without their knowledge or permission as this is quite separate from the DNA profiling carried out on a sample taken only for that reason?

SUMMARY

There is a complexity in ethical questions which has not in itself been adequately addressed. In the past it has been the objective of philosophers to produce general frameworks within which all societies can operate for mutual benefit. What this fails to take into account is the increasing technical complexity of our society, which brings with it questions of a unique nature that cannot be easily described or solved using reasoning from an era which could not conceive of our technological based society. At the same time, we should not shy away from asking difficult questions, just because there are no straight forward or obvious solutions.

If we are to make the most of DNA technology we have to grasp the nettle and say precisely how far we want it to go now, not wait until it has already happened. Dolly the sheep was not a surprise in the scientific community, what was a surprise was that the birth caused so much consternation, but so little consideration amongst legislative bodies that they simply put a 'patch' on already present regulations without thinking the entire question through. It is for us all to decide upon these new technologies and how they are to be applied, not a small group of scientists or politicians. What happens now will not necessarily affect us, but might well affect future generations, for good or bad. It is up to us now to see that it is for good.

APPENDIX

A NOTE ON STATISTICAL INFERENCES

Statistics is about taking measurements, of any sort, and using them to create a model which has some predictive power. There would be little sense in setting up a model on data which is misleading, such as all cows have four legs, the kitchen table has four legs therefore it is a cow. The data must be sensibly applicable. Because we tend to create models of the world around us and apply the data we tend to forget that this is what we do all the time, so we recognise a cow as fitting our idea of a cow and a table our idea of a table. Where our internal models can fall down are situations that are either unique, or where the model is inaccurate. An example of this would a child be trying to decide what group of animals a duck-billed platypus belongs to; it is furry, but lays eggs, it has webbed feet and a beak, but suckles its young. Without a frame-work to put such an animal in it is difficult to decide what it is.

Statistics are designed to help with such problems, but on a slightly more abstract level. If we have new drug we want to know if it will work in the way we think it will, but not everyone reacts to a drug in the same way, so we have to take a large selection of people and give them the drug to see what happens. If we are very lucky all the tested individuals will react in the same way to the same dose, a situation never likely to occur. So what is needed is a method of sorting results such that we can find out if overall there is a pattern of response which can then be used as a model for treatment.

In forensic applications this takes the form of setting up databases and tests to see how predictive any given result, in the form of a DNA profile is, of pin-pointing an individual. There are several basic methods of doing this, but it is more the expression of the results which are of interest because what they appear to say may not be what they actually mean.

CORRELATIONS

The most straightforward method of relating two variables together is that of correlation. This is a statistical process which takes the data from a simple graph of two variables. So we could measure height against weight and expect a clear relationship, but there would always be people who were obese or thin, so the correlation would not be exact. A case where an exact correlation can be found is, say, between the price of apples and the amount bought, 10 kilos will cost exactly twice that of five kilos.

Such precise and exact correlations are relatively rare in statistical analysis. A case where the correlation was exact would be referred to as having a correlation (r) of one, so perfect positive correlation is:

$$r = +1$$

The converse is also true, when one item is negatively correlated with another, we find that the correlation is negative:

$$r = -1$$

Sadly, this situation is very rarely encountered, if it were, then knowing one value would mean that we could exactly determine the other value. As can be easily appreciated, if correlations range from +1 to –1, a value of 0 means there is no relationship, so knowing one value can tell us nothing about the other.

Having any value other than zero for a correlation implies that if we know one value we can say something about the other value with which it is correlated. The greater the value of the correlation, the more accurate the prediction of one value from the other becomes.

Unfortunately for a lay observer the intuitive interpretation of a correlation is not necessarily correct. A correlation is not a proportion; a correlation of 0.6 does not represent a relationship twice as great as 0.3. Worse! The difference between a correlation of 0.4 and 0.5 is not the same as between 0.5 and 0.6.

What the correlation does tell us can most simply be stated as a relationship with a twist; if we square the correlation and multiply by 100 we produce a meaningful figure. Take an example of a correlation of 0.5. Square this (0.5 x 0.5 = 0.25) and multiply this by 100. Result 25%, so we know 25% of what we would need to know to make a perfect prediction of one value from another.

It should also be remembered that having a correlation coefficient does not imply a causal relationship, it may be functional, that is, the two measurements may appear to be causally linked, but are in fact functionally linked together, both being causally linked to a third variable.

PROBABILITY

Probability is the area of statistics which is most often seen in forensic cases, and, as discussed earlier in this book, can sometimes be better stated as odds, as used in betting. This does, however, have the drawback of appearing to try and foresee the future. This is at the most subjective end of probability.

A second usage of probability is found in strict mathematical analysis of situations where analysis is made of the probability ratio of a favourable outcome compared to the total number of equally likely cases. This is a convoluted way of saying the probability of simple games of chance, dealing an ace from a pack of cards or tossing a dice and getting, say, a three. Since there are six sides to a dice and each is equally likely, throwing a three is 1/6. This is a useful method of modelling some events, but in forensic applications it is another application of probability which is of most use.

For most applications of probability in legal cases it is a consideration of relative frequencies which is the most useful. This takes the form of making repeated measurements (N) in the form of DNA profiles and then saying that a specified profile occurs 'r' times, so the relative frequency is r/N. What has traditionally been done with such data is to then give a confidence interval for the result. This is one of the most counter-intuitive ideas which appears in statistics and one which causes the greatest confusion.

A confidence interval may be stated as 95%, now logically and intuitively, it would be assumed that this meant that the value we have, the probability of two profiles matching, say, would have a 95% probability of being correct. But this is not so. What it actually tells us is that repeating the procedure would result in the unknown being within my parameters of measurement 95% of the time. Not very useful information. Put another way, we would reject the null hypothesis that the two profiles were different 95% of the time. As can be readily appreciated, this would not be a very helpful piece of information to the court, if only because there are only two profiles under consideration. A different way of looking at these results was required and as it turned out was already available.

There is another way of interpreting data which does not require this convoluted appraisal. Although much developed it is still referred to as

Bayesian statistics, after the Presbyterian minister Thomas Bayes who first suggested this way of analysing statistical data. An intriguing point here is why he should have been so interested in statistics in the first place. He did produce a considerable bulk of work, but virtually none of it was published under his own name in his lifetime. His theories were readily accepted at the time of publication, but were later seen as rather subjective by later statisticians. To think this theory subjective is a mistake. It may at first seem that way, but closer examination will show us differently.

What he managed to do was essentially turn the classical statistical ideas upside down. Instead of the apparently objective classical method of making a calculation and assigning a probability to it, the Bayesian method produced a result depending on what the experimenter believed. It is said to be an apparently objective method because the point at which the experimenter decides that the results are significant is entirely up to the experimenter to decide, which can often be rather arbitrary.

With Bayesian statistics the final result is worked out by producing a likelihood and multiplying the result by your prior beliefs. This can be quite difficult in the context of a forensic calculation, but it is almost certainly what a jury will do. The result is that when a Bayes confidence interval is stated as 95%, it really does mean a point at which you would be justified in thinking that 95% of the time that is where the results will lay.

A major difference between classical statistics and Bayesian statistics is one of the fundamental reasons that this latter technique is best suited to forensic applications. In classical situations the hypothesis which is tested is based upon possible outcomes, that is, what may or may not have happened. In Bayesian statistics it is only the observed result which is relevant, which when you consider it, is a self-evident truth. It is the match between DNA profiles which we are interested in, not the probability that they might or might not match, should a comparison be made.

FURTHER READING

DNA VARIATION AND ITS HISTORICAL CONTEXT

Ciba Foundation Symposium 197, 'Variation in the human genome', 1996, Chichester: John Wiley

McCarty, M, *The Transforming Principle: Discovering That Genes Are Made of DNA*, 1986, New York: WW Norton & Co

Watson, JD, *The Double Helix*, 1970, London: Penguin

FINGERPRINTS AND BERTILLONAGE

Bertillon, A, *La Photographie Judiciaire*, 1890, Paris: G Masson

Cole, SA, *Suspect Identities: A History of Fingerprinting and Criminal Identification*, 2001, Cambridge, Mass: Harvard UP

Evett, I and Williams, R, *A Review of the Sixteen Points Fingerprint Standard in England and Wales*, 1989, London: Crown Copyright

Galton, F, *Finger Prints*, 1892, London: MacMillan

Wall, WJ, 'From here to infinity' (2000) 47 Biologist 56

STATISTICS AND INTERPRETATION OF RESULTS

Balding, D and Donnelly, P, 'The prosecutor's fallacy and DNA' (October 1994) Evidence Crim LR

Boyle, D, *The Tyranny of Numbers*, 2001, London: HarperCollins

DNA Technology and Forensic Science, Banbury Report 32, 1989, New York: Cold Spring Harbour

Hogg, RV and Tanis, EA, *Probability and Statistical Inference*, 1977, London: Collier MacMillan

Lander, ES, 'DNA fingerprinting on trial' (1989) 339 Nature 501–05

Lee, PM, *Bayesian Statistics: An Introduction*, 1989, London: Arnold

Robertson, B and Vignaux, GA, *Interpreting Evidence*, 1995, Chichester: John Wiley

EXPERTS AND ALL THEY PURPORT TO BE

Bond, C, Solon, M and Harper, P, *The Expert Witness in Court*, 1997, Kent: Shaw and Sons

DNA Technology in Forensic Science, 1992, Washington: National Academy

Hall, JG and Graham, DS, *The Expert Witness*, 1992, Chichester: Barry Rose

INDEX

E

T

V

W